NEVER TO LOSE MY VISION

NEVER TO LOSE MY VISION
The story of Bill Jaeger

by
CLARA JAEGER

Grosvenor Books

First published 1995
GROSVENOR BOOKS
54 Lyford Road
London SW18 3JJ

Suite 500, 251 Bank Street
Ottawa, Ontario K2P 1X3
Canada

226 Kooyong Road
Toorak, VIC 3142
Australia

PO Box 1834, Wellington
New Zealand

GROSVENOR USA
3735 Cherry Avenue NE
Salem, Oregon 97303

British Library Cataloguing-in-publication Data:
A catalogue record of this book is available
from the British Library

ISBN 1 85239 022 0

Book design: Blair Cummock
Cover design: Dell Williams
Cover photograph: Philip Carr

Typeset in Sabon 11pt by Blair Cummock, Tirley Garth, Cheshire, UK
Printed by Biddles Ltd, Guildford, England

Dedication

Following is an alphabetical list of those who worked with Bill over the years. And it is to them that I dedicate this book:

Joy and Frank Abbott
Jap and Riek de Boer
Warner Clark
Sydney and Linde Cook
Duncan and Lucy Corcoran
Dick and Margaret Cosens
Betty Cook
Dorothy Ensor
Geoffrey and Jeanette Gain
Tom and Liz Gillespie
Charles and Margery Haines
David and Gail Hind
Joe and Karen Hodgson
Paul Hogue
David and Suzanne Howell
June Lee
Ian and Pauline Maclachlan
Andrew and Jean Mackay
George 'Scotty' Macfarlane
Finlay and Kath Moir
François and Nicole Maunoir

Daniel and Monique Mottu
Jean-Jacques and Marie-Lise Odier
Molly Orchard
David and Janny Peters
Alec and Alison Porter
William E Porter
Luis and Evelyn Puig
Blyth and Edith Ramsay
Ian and Kitty Rae
Don and Connie Simpson
Stuart and Polly Ann Smith
Eric Turpin
Laurie and Elsa Vogel
George and Rosamund Vondermuhll
George and Gwyneth Walker
Don and Connie Weight
Gordon and Marjory Wise

Acknowledgments

First mention must go to Hugh Nowell who bravely stepped out in faith and said he would work for the publication of the book even though it was clear to him from the beginning that it would be a difficult thing to capture the essence of my husband's long life. And to the Grosvenor Books team who finally realised this dream.

Other supporters from the early days are the Wise family – Gordon, Marjory and Gordon Scott. Gordon, who worked alongside my husband for so many years, has continued to give encouragement, advice and contributions through the many long months as we went through various stages.

Then, my heartfelt thanks to Elizabeth Locke who, when she saw the early manuscript, set certain goals, steering me bit by bit into a streamlined narrative.

Thirdly, I was blessed with the gift of a brilliant editor in the person of Virginia Wigan, who lived with great sensitivity into what I was trying to express, yet honed and polished, researched and marshalled the intricate comings and goings of a life spanning 80 years.

I want to thank Peter and Margaret Sisam for agreeing to take on the photographs, and choosing just the right ones, and for the skilled workmanship they brought to the finished products.

Thanks also to Dell Williams for agreeing to do the cover for the book, and tracking down the right photograph for it.

Thanks too to Blair Cummock, a true artist in book design.

And I want very much to thank the many friends of Bill's to whom I wrote asking for memories of working with him, and facts and figures that were needed to tell the story. I am giving their names alphabetically:

Frank and Joy Abbott, Duncan and Lucy Corcoran, Sydney and Linde Cook, Geoffrey Gain, Tom and Liz Gillespie, Bryan Hamlin, James Hore-Ruthven, David and Suzanne Howell, Stanley Kiaer, Frank Ledwith, Pauline Maclachlan, Archie Mackenzie, Adam McLean, Daniel Mottu, James Newton, Alec Porter, Blyth and Edith Ramsay, Richard Ruffin, Don Simpson, Stuart and Polly Ann Smith, Eric Turpin, George Vondermuhll, Gordon and Marjory Wise, John and Denise Wood.

And now to thank the person who started it all, Anne Elisabeth Suter. She, too, had faith, and I certainly thank her for getting me going.

Clara Jaeger

Contents

Introduction

Bill Jaeger was 29 when I met him for the first time in 1941 in Connecticut. We were hard at work when there was a loud commotion at the back of the hall. Suddenly everyone dashed off to meet four newcomers, one of whom turned out to be Bill. I'd been really curious to meet him, though I wasn't sure why. I joined the circle around him, and looked with interest at the person so many people had tried to describe to me.

He was short and stocky, and was wearing an old raincoat, a bent hat crushed down on his head, and carrying an armful of newspapers. He had observant blue eyes, a rather large, straight nose, a firm jutting chin, and a manner which had a warm greeting for everyone. I wasn't sure if I liked him or not ... but there was a certain authority about him.

A young British student met Bill almost half a century later, at a 1990 political party conference in the south of England: 'He could have just said "hello" to me after he'd heard me speak that day, but he didn't. He picked me out and greeted me with genuine interest and friendliness. My life has changed ever since.'

Fred Small who was Vice-President of the Longshoremen of Brooklyn, New York, said: 'Bill is one of the best informed foreigners I have met. He understands the inner workings of people. As far as labour and trade unions are concerned, he is a senior statesman. You can tell him anything and his advice is always good. I'm just glad he is my friend.'

Francis Blanchard, former Director-General of the ILO, said: 'Nothing that concerns the world of work, and even wider, the condition of the men and women of our time, is foreign to him. His curiosity of spirit is boundless – as is his generosity and his compassion for all those who suffer.'

I once confided to my diary: 'It is hard to put a label on Bill. I think his background of poverty fashioned a character which is not only steadfast and dependable, but generous and full of humour as well.'

This is the story of a most unusual man, from an ordinary street in the industrial heart of England ...

I

Stockport

Stockport, near Manchester, England, 1912

His roots were in that part of England whose social injustices had fired the thinking of Marx and Engels, where England's working classes eked out an existence in what became known as 'the dark satanic mills'*. He came from there and would always be proud of his working class background. And though he was to travel to all five continents of the world, he never forgot those roots, and the grimmer side of life which he had witnessed and lived through as a boy.

The street where he lived, an only child, with his parents, was lined with rows of small, dingy dwellings and shops. The only colour came from the signs outside the many public houses (pubs) that were all around the area – *The Old Ram's Head*, *The Flying Dutchman*, *The Shakespeare* – named after racehorses. Others were *The Royal Mortar*, *The Star*, and *The Blossoms*. People went in and out from them all the time. The streets were paved with cobblestones. There were no trees within three miles.

The Jaeger home was in the centre of industry. It had a small back yard, an area paved with tiles. The WC was there. Directly behind was a factory where 400 girls

* William Blake's hymn, 'Jerusalem'

worked, and to the right was a brewery from which the froth from the beer would blow up and down the footpath. Farther along was Christie's hat factory, where they employed several hundred men and women to make and trim men's and ladies' velour hats which were sent out all over the world. To the left was Smith's cotton mill, where they made towels and produced reels of cotton.

In the days when Annie and Charles Jaeger first lived there, everyone wore clogs, and the women wore shawls. The day started at six, when the 'knocker-up' came by to get people on the way to the mills.

One memory that never left him was the scenes on Saturday night, when women were carried out drunk from the pubs and left on the pavement to join their crying children. They had purchased a few hours of oblivion through gin for a couple of pennies. Sometimes a figure would lurch against the Jaeger shop window and break the glass.

* * * * *

Stockport is only seven miles from the great manufacturing city of Manchester, an area that typified perhaps more than any other in England the ravages and cruel injustices brought into a once rural area by the industrial revolution.

In the latter part of the nineteenth century Archibald Prentice, a leader of the anti-Corn Law Movement, cited visits to 258 families consisting of 1,009 individuals, whose average earnings were seven-and-a-half pennies a week. Children of five years old and upward worked in the factories, usually for 12 hours a day, often for 14 or 16 hours.

Not infrequently they worked through the night. Some were caught in the unfenced machinery and terribly injured. Others fell victim to the various forms of tuberculosis caused by the dirt-laden atmosphere of the mills. The children snatched their food as they worked, because during the official meal breaks it was their job to clean the machinery. Hungry and exhausted towards the end of the day they fell asleep at their work, only to be roused by the overseer's whip.

Friedrich Engels, the German socialist and close colleague of Karl Marx, arrived in Manchester in late 1842, and vividly described his impressions of one of the worst areas:*

'The race that lives in these ruinous cottages behind broken windows, mended in oilskin, sprung doors, and rotten doorposts, or in dark, wet cellars, in measureless filth and stench, in this atmosphere penned in as if with a purpose... must really have reached the lowest stage of humanity. In each of these pens, containing at most two rooms, a garret and perhaps a cellar, on the average 20 human beings live.'

One Englishman who was shocked into taking action was Anthony Ashley Cooper, Seventh Earl of Shaftesbury. Born into privilege, he could have spent his life well insulated from the lives of the working classes, but he engaged in a tireless battle to pass laws through Parliament that would provide some protection for the poor, and especially for the children.

Beginning in 1833, Shaftesbury's Factory Acts freed all children under nine, restricted youngsters under 13 to 6+ hours' work a day and young persons and women to 60 hours a week with no night work.

There was a period of only 37 years between Shaftesbury's final act being passed in Parliament and William Jaeger's birth into that northern industrial area in 1912.

* * * * *

William's mother, Annie Day, was introduced as a child to the hat-renovating business which her parents had started. Her father and mother had met in the warehouse of a hat-making firm, the father blocking hats and the mother designing samples to be copied. Annie often worked in the family's shop from eight in the morning until ten at night, and she loved it.

The Condition of the Working Class in England, Engels

She was a lively, spirited, very pretty girl, with thick blonde hair, always nicely dressed. She was the eldest of four children, and was depended on very much by her mother to bring in money through her wages.

Choral singing was very popular in that part of England during those years. The choir provided a social milieu for boys and girls to meet. Annie joined one of the choirs, and it was there she met her future husband.

Charles Jaeger was born in Liverpool, but his father came from Germany. Charles was a gifted man, a skilled cabinet maker, and employed at a respectable salary before his marriage by Waring & Gillow, a well-known furniture firm. He painted landscapes, and was also extremely musical, playing the piano and the violin. He even made a violin of his own.

Charles had a strong, clear tenor voice, and it was this voice, soaring over all others, that first attracted Annie when he joined her choir.

Singing was their great delight, and their choir was distinguished enough to join a choir festival in the Royal Albert Hall in London.

Charles courted Annie for seven years, but she was afraid to accept him because her mother strongly disapproved of the young man's German name. Finally Charles gave an ultimatum: accept or say goodbye. She accepted.

* * * * *

William liked to explain that he was born in a hatshop, which is indeed true, since after their marriage his parents set up in business for themselves, dying and re-shaping hats. This was all done on their small premises, with the dying vats in the back yard. They called the shop 'The Old Firm'. Most of the business was to clean and re-shape hats, for which the charge was two shillings and ninepence. If they were to be dyed, it cost a further shilling.

Annie was 37 years old when William was born. She was attended by a young Indian doctor named Gandhi. It

16

was the first time he had delivered a baby. It turned out to be a difficult birth, as the baby had a really large head.

In William's early years a number of episodes etched themselves deeply into the boy's subconscious, to reappear at intervals through his life.

His father bought him a rabbit, the only pet William ever had, and the only animal he ever had the chance to know. But one morning when he went out to feed it, he found that rats had attacked and killed it.

One day the chimney of the house next door caught fire, and the sparks flew onto the Jaeger premises. After some effort they were put out, but a fear of house fires was implanted in the boy which was never to leave him.

During those childhood years, Britain was at war with Germany, and when he was four William first encountered racism, because of his German name. Often when the family went out on the street people would shout at them. One day William was knocked off his small tricycle by some children who called him a dirty little German.

'Am I a dirty little German?' the small boy asked his parents.

'Well, what if you are?' responded his father.

'I shouldn't mind if you and mother were, too,' William answered.

The persecution intensified. One morning a neighbour came into the shop to warn them that a crowd of people was on its way to smash their windows. Charles went to the police to report it, and for the next two years they lived under police protection.

As the war with Germany dragged on, bogged down in the mud and barbed wire of Northern France, Britain looked for more men to replace the non-stop drain on her armies. Men of 45 were called up, Charles Jaeger among them. His doctor had sent a request for exemption due to health reasons, but the letter was misplaced and never got to the examiners. He was given a very severe test, and at

17

the end was completely exhausted. For a while he had to be treated in hospital, which used up a sizeable amount of his precious savings. It was the beginning of a kind of nervous breakdown for Charles which gradually intensified through William's childhood years.

But by far the most disturbing experience of those early days was the realisation that his parents were governed by fear about money, or rather the lack of it.

Annie always understood that the Jaegers, Charles's brothers and sisters and mother, had some money. She knew Charles put his salary away in the bank, though he had never told her how much he actually earned.

Their arrangement was that Charles would pay the rent and rates, but everything else was to come out of money brought in through the shop. Annie was responsible for this part of their lives.

All went well for a number of years, but then business slackened, and the weekly incomings became really meagre. Yet Annie was still expected to pay all the bills and feed and clothe the family.

She was too proud to ask her husband for money, although she kept accounts carefully and he was well aware how little she had. Charles was worried about the future, which was why he held onto what money they had in the bank. But, caught between her pride and fear, Annie began to turn on her husband when he blamed her for the fact that so little was coming into the shop.

William came home one half-closing day to find his parents having a blazing row. He saw his father strike his mother, and Annie fleeing the house, saying she was 'going to the pond', to drown herself. Shock and terror struck the boy's heart. Though his mother did not carry out her threat, the memory of those harsh words never left him. Violent quarrels happened often throughout his childhood. 'It tore my guts,' he said.

Painful experiences like these played a large part in shaping his character. He handled them by resolutely

18

pushing them down. It became his nature to fight on and be positive, almost to discount any issue that could cause him pain. A boy like him from the poor side of town soon realised he could not afford to give in.

*   *   *   *   *

Charles was anxious that William get a good education, and when he was six he entered him in a well-known private school. Mindful of the threats being made against them, Charles would not allow William to make the school journey alone, but walked him there and back.

When he was nine, his father entered him in Stockport Grammar School, which had been founded in 1487 by the then Lord Mayor of London, Sir Edward Shaa.

As a child, William was short for his age. He had a large head, high forehead, large eyes and a firm, almost jutting chin, a large straight nose and thick dark hair. He loved to argue, and a mixture of stubbornness and pride meant that he was never prepared to lose an argument – he had to prove that he was right. However, he was the apple of his parents' eyes, and had a close relationship with them.

Eric Broadbent, a next-door neighbour, recalled the childhood days in Stockport:

'From the age of eight or nine I spent an increasing amount of hours, particularly on wet days, with William, who introduced me to various indoor games, such as table bowls and book cricket. A good deal of organising was involved, in drawing up championship tables, or batting and bowling averages for the teams and players who were notionally taking part. In this William was in his element. Later he became a keen and vigorous tennis player.' He also played a lot of chess.

From an early age William followed the national sport of football, reading up about the matches in the newspapers. It became a lifelong passion.

*   *   *   *   *

19

When William arrived home from school the family would have the main meal of the day, which they called tea. Lots of tea to drink, bread, pikelets (a kind of crumpet), some fish or an egg, perhaps some chips. It was a special treat on Sundays to have any fruit, or meat which was often in the form of rabbit. Tripe was a staple of their diet.

Directly across the street was a fish and chip shop, and sometimes William would go over and buy two penny-worth of chips, no fish, and return home with them to douse them with vinegar. It was a favourite meal.

Sundays were very full: Sunday School at the local Baptist Church at 9.30, then church, then back again after dinner for Sunday School at 2.30, then church again in the evening.

For financial reasons, and like most of their neighbours, they never went to a dentist, and only to a doctor in dire emergencies.

*　　*　　*　　*　　*

Father and son were very close. Charles started taking William to political meetings, where he became familiar with the set-up of the local political bodies.

William had a thirst for knowledge, especially about politics and the power structure of the world. From the age of about eight he read everything he could get his hands on, and developed a wide range of interests.

Lloyd George was Prime Minister, and Charles was a staunch member of his Liberal Party. Imagine the shock William had one day when he discovered that the Tory *Daily Mail* had been delivered in error to the house. He snatched it up and hurried along to the newspaper shop and demanded *The News Chronicle*, the Liberal paper they always took.

His early interests were those of a mature person, and his ability to study and learn quickly meant he could carry on conversations with much older people.

His mother took him along with her when she went to

20

attend the Salvation Army meetings. Sometimes Annie was asked to sing a solo there, and William would accompany her on the piano. Music came as a natural inheritance to the boy. He more or less taught himself to play the instruments in their small house – the piano and the harmonium. He had a retentive memory. In his mid teens he memorised the first movement of Beethoven's First Symphony, and could play an arrangement of it on the piano.

A noticeable trait in his personality was his ability for friendship – the way he wanted to speak to people. He had a sensitive awareness of what others were feeling. He noticed them when passing them on the street, and gave a friendly nod or lifted his cap. He liked to visit the shops and homes along the way and have a chat.

His own home constantly had people dropping in; first perhaps to make a small purchase, but staying on to talk to Charles and Annie about what was going on in the town. The Salvation Army people were frequent visitors, and also the Quakers, equally concerned about the social conditions. The young boy listened, all ears, absorbing and remembering.

*   *   *   *   *

It was a formative moment in his life when, at the age of 13, he was baptised and taken into the Baptist Church. He understood, even at that age, that he was meant to live what he later described as a life of service.

In Stockport in those days inter-church Bible competitions took place. A subject was set, for instance 'The Acts', and a written examination given to any who would like to compete. William won the competition three years running, with marks of 100%, and was given 'The Shield'.

He was 16 when he was first asked to preach. He had grown up in the churchgoing atmosphere provided by his parents. But so far as he could judge, churchgoers left little impact on the serious problems in the town.

At 16 William was a popular school prefect. He took an

21

active part in the Debating Society and French Society. With his headmaster he produced a school orchestra of 40 members, students and teachers. They gave a concert, and William was the conductor. It was quite an emotional event for Annie, sitting in the audience, watching the young conductor, with 'the perspiration pouring down his face and his tie flapping about', anxious in case William gave the wrong beat.

Like all boys at a certain point he became very aware of girls. He joined the lads standing on the street corners watching the girls go by. He noticed what the girls looked like, which ones were pretty, but always from a distance. He admitted to noticing one girl in particular and following her at a safe distance to see where she lived. But he never summoned up the courage to talk to her.

He was happy enough at home with his father and mother in the evenings, playing the piano and reading, reading, reading. There was so much he wanted to know.

* * * * *

During William's final year in school, his father's health began to deteriorate markedly. Charles had a stay of 16 weeks in a nursing home, and after coming home he presented a changed personality. He was deeply withdrawn, and difficult for Annie to look after. Gone was the warm, outgoingness to others which had so marked him before. The only way he came to life at all was through music. William discovered that when he played the piano, his father would take up his violin and join in. Father and son passed many hours together in this way.

Then one day Charles ate some mackerel that was not fresh, resulting in ptomaine poisoning. Over the next months he was in and out of hospital, examined by four specialists, but steadily weakened. Finally he developed aplastic anaemia, for which there was no cure in those days, and this it was that killed him.

22

His father's death altered William's life overnight. At 19 he changed from a boy to a man.

Charles' will left his money to his wife and son, but it had been largely depleted by hospital bills. Just before he died he said to Annie, 'I know you will use what money is left rightly, and I know you won't let anything stand in William's way.'

*   *   *   *   *

During his father's last illness, they had often discussed what career William might choose for his life's work. Because of his good grades at school he felt encouraged to let his imagination wander a bit; might it be, for instance, a scholarship to study history at Oxford? Or a career in music? But his thoughts would always return to the church, in which work he had already been active, and in which, he realised, his parents hoped he might make his life work.

He applied to a number of Baptist colleges, finally settling on Regent's Park Baptist college in London. His headmaster arranged an interview for him, saying, 'He is a boy of whom I can hardly speak too highly.' William passed the entrance exam, and early in September, 1931, the day of departure came.

The small case he packed was quite adequate for the few clothes he took with him. He wore his school blazer. He had never before been further away from Stockport than Liverpool, where his father's relatives lived. Now he was headed for London.

It was a proud moment for Annie, and equally a poignant one. How quiet the little home would be without his lively presence. William well understood the feelings of his mother, but being what they both were, no feelings were expressed on either side. Goodbye was quite matter-of-fact, and suddenly he was gone.

II

Setting a course

With characteristic thoroughness and enthusiasm, William settled down to his religious studies: Psychology, Logic, Church History, the New Testament, Greek, Hebrew, Philosophy, Comparative Religious Studies and other kindred courses.

Also, equally characteristically, by the end of his first week he had become friendly with several fellow students. One day one of them said to him, 'Why don't you come along and meet some interesting people I know; I think you will like them.'

William not only liked the people he was taken to meet, but was captivated by the ideas they put forth. They belonged to 'The Oxford Group', whose informal membership numbered many hundreds around the world. Their aim, they said, was to build a better society for everybody, regardless of race, class or nationality – in short, they said, 'to remake the world'.

The basic starting point was helpfully specific – the readiness of each person to make real in their own lives the qualities they wanted to see in society. The group's American initiator, Dr Frank Buchman, adopted four guidelines, standards, by which to test one's motives and actions: absolute honesty, absolute purity, absolute unselfishness and absolute love.

Then, after honest self-appraisal in these four areas, they

suggested a time of meditation, to take heed of the promptings deep within – the inner voice of God, or just simply one's conscience. Some thoughts might come as a result of this – thoughts, they observed, that if written down could be remembered and acted upon.

These clear directions really hooked William's imagination, to the extent that he found he was impatient to get away by himself and to assess his life in the light of the four standards they mentioned.

There did not seem to be any lurid or dramatic sins to acknowledge. But, he recalled, he had once accepted help from a friend in one of his Greek exams, and he decided he would go and tell his professor about it. Also, it might be better if he was not so argumentative with his mother. Perhaps he was too self-sufficient.

Ever since the day he had been baptised at the age of 13 William had a simple, unquestioning faith in God. But so far he had not worked out how it could be adequately related to actual needs, social as well as personal. Now he completely accepted the importance of personal change. Equally he quickly grasped the fact that this was only a first step. By itself it was not enough. His mind burned with a desire to see this concept applied to what he felt were the social evils all around him every day. He reflected on the problems which had always distressed him in Stockport – the sad, bitter faces in the streets, the broken homes, the many gambling and drinking establishments.

The simple yet profound approach of the Oxford Group seemed to make effective the work he had always wanted to do – to help people. It really was not a departure, but a development of the work he had felt called to do since his baptism at the age of 13. His aim could be summed up in two questions: how can we build a better society for everybody, and can people ever live to the full what they talk about?

Waking up the next morning he felt filled with a new energy and freedom, and a great desire to tell someone

26

about what he felt was an important discovery. He found one of his theological student friends and described it all to him. The young man was very moved to hear William's honesty, and in turn confided in William about the real problems in his own life.

From that day forward William had a compulsion to pass on the vision he had, of what the world might become if people would take the steps he and hundreds of others had taken.

*   *   *   *   *

After her son had gone to London, Annie at times found herself assailed by fears, alone in her small shop. She knew there was very little money left in the bank, some of which she would need to send on to William for his expenses. Hats could be bought cheaper elsewhere now. Much competition came from the large stores in the town. She was living on her dwindling capital.

She said nothing to William about the situation, not wanting to distract him from his studies. Success in his work would be a source of comfort to them both.

But she was counting the days until he would come home for the holidays.

*   *   *   *   *

When he arrived home for that Christmas of 1931, he seemed to burst into the house, bringing with him a whirlwind of enthusiasm and vitality. Over tea Annie asked all the questions she had been saving up about life in college and his studies.

However, after half an hour or so, the conversation took a different turn.

'Mother,' said William, 'why didn't you tell me of the things I would be up against in a city like London, the temptations I would be faced with?'

Annie was both taken aback and almost embarrassed by this frankness. Relationships between boys and girls, for instance, were strictly not mentioned in the home.

When William went on to tell her about the four standards of the Oxford Group, Annie became not only uncomfortable but quite angry. After all, for 40 years she had taken an active part in the church, and taught in Sunday School.

'That's all right for young people,' she responded, 'but I don't need it.'

William, unruffled, told her how it helped to write down the thoughts that came after going over those standards. Her reaction was that it seemed 'stupid'.

Again William persisted, drawing his mother out, asking questions. The hours went by, and they talked together as they had never talked before.

It was almost two o'clock in the morning when William suggested they might now be quiet together and just see what thoughts might come into each of their minds.

After a few moments of silence, Annie had one clear thought: to be honest about finances. And so she told him the real situation they were in. Having come clean, she immediately felt a wonderful relief and release from fear.

And so, about three o'clock in the morning, mother and son got down on their knees in the little back room and each prayed to God and gave him their lives to use as he would. Annie rose with her heart seeming to sing with joy because besides the new openness with her son, she felt that somehow each of them now had a great task to perform.

*　　*　　*　　*　　*

The day after this talk with William she was standing in the doorway of her shop when one of her neighbours passed and took a quick, second look at her face. 'Mrs Jaeger,' she enquired, 'what's happened to your face? It's different.' Annie said, 'Come inside and I'll tell you.'

28

She told her about her talk with William, about being honest and the need to start with oneself in any situation.

The neighbour said, 'Do you think I could change?' Annie replied, 'Why not? If you will listen and be honest about your deepest thoughts...' And so they were quiet together, and in a moment the neighbour said she had one thought, 'To stop nagging my husband.' She had seven children, and both she and her husband drank heavily and gambled, even being known to pawn their children's clothes to have money to spend on 'the dogs' (greyhound racing). She used to kick one of her boys when he did not do as she wanted.

Word went up and down the street about the effect of Annie's talk with this woman, and more neighbours began coming in to speak about their problems. Many went away with hope and a determination to live differently.

Annie was not alone any more, in fact her life was so full that she could hardly find enough time to keep in touch with all the people who seemed to need her care. But the truth also was that now there was so little money coming into the shop that the income had dwindled to almost nothing.

One day, in desperation, she confided in one of her friends about the true state of her finances. This friend suggested she go to a local charity and tell them the situation. This she did, and some time later the governors of the charity decided to grant her a short-term pension of seven shillings and sixpence a week.

*   *   *   *   *

For the next four years William continued his religious studies, which had now taken on a deeper meaning. He also began to study some of the literature put out by the Oxford Group. He learned it had started when Dr Frank Buchman, a Lutheran clergyman from Pennsylvania, had heard a sermon preached by a woman in a small church in the north of England. What Buchman heard made him realise that he himself was not living what he talked about, because of the bitterness he was nurturing toward six men who had thwarted him in certain plans he had. The bitterness was so intense that it had made him ill, and his doctor had suggested he should travel for his health. As the sermon came to a close, Buchman faced the fact that this bitterness had cut him off from God. He wrote and apologised to the six men for nurturing ill-will against them.

The same afternoon he told another man about the truth he had found. The simple, far-reaching experience developed and grew through the next 20 years as he gathered a group around him, and found himself travelling the world.

*   *   *   *   *

For William it was a natural progression quickly to become involved with the activities of the Oxford Group, and he travelled several times to the large meetings being held at colleges in Oxford, where there were speakers from many other countries – Canada, the United States, Sweden, Denmark, South Africa, Germany.

Geoffrey Gain, a fellow student, first met William at a meeting in Oxford:

'One hot Sunday evening in July, 1933, I bumped into Bill Jaeger. We both said "Sorry!", and then grinned as we followed the crowd out of the Oxford College Hall, where one of the meetings had just ended.

'Outside I could see Jaeger better, but I never guessed that I was looking at a man who for the next six years was going to have a revolutionary influence on my life.

'He was a craggy-looking fellow, with a head like a mastiff's and thick, untidy hair. He wore a blazer with a crest and yellow stripes. "Stockport Grammar School," he said proudly, giving the crest a thump; "My name's Jaeger, what's yours?" I told him. "What do you do?" he asked ... "Office work? Student?" I said I was just about to become a student at a certain college. "Why", he said, "that's my college. I've been there for a year. Now you're coming too. It's good we have met like this."

'In the next three years I saw Jaeger develop a spiritual generalship of a high order. While he was still a student many men of widely different backgrounds and experience were looking to him for advice and help in all kinds of business and home problems.

'We learned together. Bill asked me one day, "Do you know anything about the trade unions?" "Well," I answered, "I was reading something about them in yesterday's paper. Important, aren't they?" "I think they may be," was his response. "We should probably find out more."

'Bill and I saved up for a fortnight and one pouring wet Sunday in 1937 we took the day excursion to Stockport. We arrived at the family's little shop just in time for Sunday dinner.

'Bill's mother was just as I had imagined her to be – white-haired, fragile-looking but wiry; work-worn but lively.

'Even the hats and handkerchiefs and reels of coloured cotton could not make the shop bright. For its paint was faded and it looked what it was – a milliner's that had seen better days. The living-room was full of knick-knacks – little cups and statues and ornaments. And photographs everywhere. Photographs of men with beards and stand-up collars; of ladies in black dresses; and of Bill himself and his father and mother. There was a harmonium too, and a violin that Bill's father used to play. And piles of music.

'While his mother dished up the dinner, Bill sat down at the harmonium – he called it "the organ" – and began to play with great vigour. He played "Bridgebuilders", the first Oxford Group song, which had just been published. "Listen Mother," he called, "this is how it goes...."

'Before dinner was over visitors began to arrive – neighbours, relations, old school friends. Each of them began in the same way – "Hello, Bill, we heard you were coming.

How's things in London?" Soon the little room was full to overflowing. Bill began teaching his friends the new song and telling them stories from the work of the Oxford Group in London. Then he began to ask the questions – "What's your programme for changing Stockport? Have you talked to your next-door neighbour about it yet? What people are you aiming to help this week?"'

*　　*　　*　　*　　*

During the last year of his Baptist College training, William had a student pastorate north of London, in the village of Leavesden, near Watford. His sermons were quite fiery and rousing, and doubled the congregation. He clearly was a young preacher with a mission, and he set out to stir people and enlist them. William was now able to baptise people and bury them – ceremonies he was quite often called upon to perform.

But simultaneously with his church duties, William was caught up in an active Oxford Group work in North London, centring around a group of businessmen who lived not far from his college. Meetings to enlist new people were regularly taking place, often held in their homes.

William wrote to his mother:

'I have never had to work so hard in my life. I see very clearly now what I must do. I have been working along three lines. There are now about 500 men and women working with the Oxford Group in London, and it means doing personal work with them, and flinging them into action in factories, docks, offices and all kinds of places. We had a meeting of 1,200 young men in London the other week.

'Then I have been doing detailed work in East London. Several employers have asked us to speak to their employees in factories. I met 50 dockers the other week; a railway clerk invited all his office to a meeting with us in the billiard room of a public house; a gas engineer likewise arranged a meeting for his staff. The mayor of West Ham

32

1 Stockport, seven miles from the industrial city of Manchester

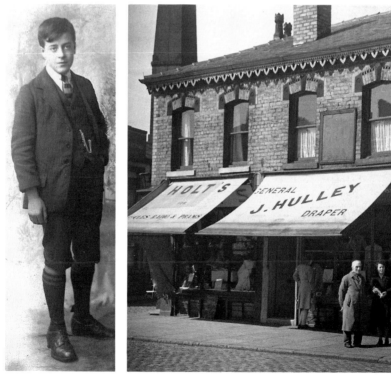

2 Bill Jaeger as a boy

3 Annie Jaeger's shop

4 East London, 'Mile after mile of little houses, each with its own smoking chimney, and countless hundreds of small shops.'

5 Bill Rowell, leader of the National Unemployed Workers' Movement, with his family.

6 Alderman Fred Welch, Deputy Mayor and later Mayor of East Ham, and his wife

is giving us an official reception in Stratford Town Hall. I had dinner with the mayor and ex-mayor of another East London borough last week.

'I have also been doing work in factories. One London employer invited 100 of his young men to go to the Oxford Group meeting in Birmingham as his guests. During the last ten days I have spent some time in Birmingham, visiting factories and meeting the men and women who work there.'

By the middle of the 1930s, the Oxford Group was beginning to draw large crowds; in 1935, 25,000 people converged at Birmingham for a mass meeting. William was involved with helping to organise some of the travel arrangements, and also practical needs such as the provision of army camp beds and blankets for the tent city erected to accommodate the visitors.

One thing William had discovered about the activities of the Oxford Group was that, whereas the majority of those affiliated with it were in regular jobs and employment, there were a number of people who were paid no salary and who gave all their time to the work. By the time he reached his final year at college, William had met a good number of these people. One was John Caulfeild, a tall, charming young man, son of a general, and who was one of Buchman's close aides at that time.

Just before William would have completed his Baptist college studies, Caulfeild asked if they could meet for a talk. He spoke on Buchman's behalf. Would he, Caulfeild asked, consider going into full-time work with the Oxford Group instead of taking a church? He suggested William might start in the East End of London, which he had already visited on a number of occasions. It was well known as an extremely tough area, with much poverty, hardship and unrest, where three million workers struggled to make a living.

William heard Caulfeild's suggestion with a surge of joy. It was almost as if he had been expecting it. He knew in

33

his bones that he had been made for just this kind of work.

He wrote to his mother:

'The thought has come to a number of people beside myself that I should begin to take on the working classes in this country, beginning in East London. I have felt quite definitely that God wanted me to do something with the working classes. To go to East London will, from the human standpoint, be difficult, for there will be no security of income. I feel, however, that this is what I am meant to do....'

Annie read the letter with mixed emotions. On the one hand she was moved by it. On the other hand, the financial uncertainty struck a well-known fear in her heart. But she wrote back saying she would accept his decision.

III

London's East End

1937

For more than 200 years, the East End had grown alongside the great metropolis of London. It stretched for miles along the river Thames.

The heart of the original East London consisted of docks and warehouses, which lay round the Pool of London on the north bank of the Thames, plus the thousands of tiny houses within walking distance, for the employees. The population had been added to from all parts of the globe – seamen jumping ship, those on the run from the law and refugees from persecution.

The smoke of 7,000 factory chimneys darkened the East London sky, with that of scores of steamers bringing raw material to the docks. There were mile after mile of little houses, each with its own smoking chimney, and countless hundreds of small shops. But by 1932 the stinking warrens described by Dickens had given way to the more accessible back-to-back dwellings.

The area was made up of 28 boroughs, each with a mayor and borough council. In the 1930s both the Communists and Fascists were hard at work in many of the toughest boroughs, fighting each other for control of the thinking and allegiance of the local population.

Most nights there were violent clashes between the

Fascists and Communists. They fought with knives and razor blades. Mounted police were sent in to try and keep the opposing groups apart, but the militants simply tipped buckets of marbles onto the paving stones so the horses were unable to keep their footing.

In 1936, when Bill was starting his full-time work with the Oxford Group, he moved to the East End, to a room in the home of the Anglican vicar of West Ham, Rev Arthur Wallace. During the first evening, while talking with his host, Bill discovered that the vicar was the chaplain to the West Ham Town Council, and was supposed to open the council sessions with prayer. However Rev Wallace admitted he had not attended the meetings for quite some time, and there and then said he would mend his ways.

He turned up at the next council meeting, and not only apologised for his irresponsibility, but told the assembled men and women, 57 Labour members and seven Conservative, that he had been reminded of this oversight after meeting some people in the Oxford Group. He went on to explain about the four absolute moral standards and was very honest about his own needs.

* * * * *

Word spread rapidly in the community about Rev Wallace being back on the job. The mayor of West Ham, a lady named Daisy Parsons, was interested to find out what had caused this change. She gave a dinner five weeks later, in a pub called *The Swan*, and invited six more mayors and deputy mayors, representing a million people from around the East End, to hear Rev Wallace, and other speakers, including Bill.

The Deputy Mayor of East Ham, Alderman Fred Welch, was so stirred by what he heard that evening that he kept saying 'Hear hear!' in a very loud voice. Bill spoke to him after the meeting, and the Alderman asked if they could have a further time to talk together, which they did the next day. Afterwards the Alderman apologised to his wife for his hurtful attitude of many years towards her, which moved her almost to tears. He also owned up that some money which was not his had found its way into his pocket.

Shortly after, Alderman Welch went to his boss and, though frightened that he might lose his job, admitted taking the money. The boss was very moved by his honesty, and wanted to know what had brought it about, indicating that he himself could use a dose of it.

At the next council meeting, the Alderman apologised to his arch enemy on the council. Up to then whenever one of them spoke, the other spoke to annoy him, even though they were in the same party. This councillor, in turn, had not spoken to the mayor of *his* borough for 18 years, and he went and apologised to him for this, leaving the man almost in a state of shock.

Bill started going every week to the council meetings and Alderman Welch would bring his friends to meet Bill. One of them was Alderman Mrs Boch, Mayor of East Ham.

She gave a dinner in a pub in East Ham called *The Denmark Arms* to which 33 of the council of 40 came. One happy result of this was that the debates and discussions on the annual rates, which used to go on interminably, with much bitter argument, now got resolved in about an hour, because the Conservative bloc supported the Socialist bloc, and vice versa, and everyone was able to go home to their families at a much earlier hour.

In the next 18 months over a hundred councils in Britain asked Alderman Welch to bring some of his council members to explain to them what had happened in the East Ham Council.

*   *   *   *   *

From the beginning Bill encouraged the new men and women recently met to go and call in other homes where they could tell their story of what had changed in their lives, and what it had meant in the home and on the job.

He set up a card index containing the names and addresses of all the people he and his team were meeting. He was thorough and painstaking. His great point was that, once met, the people must be followed up, not once but regularly; supported and helped by faithful care until they could find their feet in this new life.

At that time there was no one place where the team working with Bill in the East London area could regularly meet, which they did mornings or evenings each day. So impromptu meetings were held in schools after hours, in church halls and in the billiard rooms of pubs.

Bill's enthusiasm was infectious. In the orbit of this dynamic young man, colleagues were swept along – he made them feel that they wanted to be a part of such a great adventure. He seemed to be in love with life, this life with its great aim. There was often laughter when they met together, as Bill with practised ease drew out from his teammates what they were really thinking, and anecdotes and individual foibles saw the light of day.

His friend from college, Geoffrey Gain, was one man who joined him after completing his studies. Many others came down to the area from other parts of London, often after their paid jobs ended at five o'clock, spending the evening calling on people in their homes in the East End. Among the growing number there was a teacher from a West Ham School, an electrician, and a young man who was working in a Nursery Garden business in Surrey.

He recalled vividly the day Bill and he went out to visit someone, and stopped off at a shoe repair shop so Bill could get one of his shoes mended. While the work was being done Bill, in his socks, proceeded with great warmth of friendship to give the cobbler the assurance that his whole life could change.

News had spread around the country of the work Bill had started, beginning with himself and his first host, Rev Arthur Wallace, and of the many people in the area who had joined them in what Bill liked to call 'remaking the world'.

Bill had been working in East London about six months when one morning in 1937 Annie, in Stockport, had a startling thought: it came so clearly into her mind; was she willing to sell her home and business and join Bill? It would mean goodbye to the last bit of material security.

At first she refused to tell anyone about it. But keeping it to herself began to affect her health, and in concern some of her friends wrote to Bill, saying how unwell his mother looked. They wondered if she was hiding something.

Bill came to visit his mother, and when Annie told him the thoughts that had been troubling her he said: 'Well, mother, I'm sure God wouldn't ask you to do that unless he had some plan for you. When you are willing to accept this thought, I'm ready to take the step with you.'

*   *   *   *   *

This conversation enabled Annie to look without fear at the practical implications, and she began to open her mind to the idea that it was time for her to move out into a larger world, to get to know many more people, and to join her son in the work he had undertaken. She had never been more than 20 miles from Stockport, and she was 61 years old.

And so she sold everything, including the piano and harmonium, and all she got for her belongings was £40. She went to London, where Bill had made arrangements for her, and never again returned to her home town to live.

During his university years, Bill had been an active participant in the work of Oxford Group members living in North London, mainly businessmen, two of whom he became especially close to. One was Gordon Hassell, a director of a firm of law publishers in Chancery Lane. The other was Eric Robey, managing director of a big supplier of building materials. When Robey heard that Annie was coming to London to join Bill he suggested Bill might begin by giving her a holiday in the Robey seaside cottage in Sussex. Annie and Bill had two weeks together there, a wonderful gift to both of them.

Another family in the North London area who had grown extremely fond of Bill was that of Leonard Ball, a dentist. After hearing of Annie's arrival, they invited her to stay in their home.

Annie quickly became a beloved friend of the Hassell, Ball and Robey families; in their homes she found that her own story of how she regretted the bitterness she had nurtured against her husband, along with her self-righteousness, opened up the hearts of all three wives.

But after Bill began taking her to meet some of the dockers' wives in the East London area, she left these comfortable homes and joined her son and his band in the adventurous life of never knowing for sure where her next bed would come from.

In fact there were more requests for her to visit homes than she could accept. The word was that if Annie came to stay, somehow problems would get straightened out, especially between husband and wife, and over money.

Once Annie got started she would call on as many as 12 homes in a day, no car, of course; she walked or took a bus. There were days when Annie would go into a pub with only two pennies in her pocket and have a bun, without butter, and a cup of tea for her lunch.

'I have slept in five different homes in one week,' she wrote once.

But what East Londoners really felt when they met Bill and Annie was that they understood them, and longed to help.

Going out alone one Monday morning to do some calling, Annie knocked on the door of a large, nicely kept house. A tall, dark-haired woman opened the door and looked at her impatiently. Annie asked if she could spare a few minutes to hear about the work she was doing in the neighbourhood.

'I can't ask you in today,' the woman quickly replied, 'I'm washing. Tomorrow I'll be ironing. Wednesday I'll be cleaning upstairs and Thursday downstairs. Friday mornings I do my weekend shopping. I could be free Friday afternoon.'

Annie turned up on Friday afternoon, and was invited inside. She found the woman, Mrs Crossman, was a widow with two children, and very bitter because of the loss of her husband.

Annie told her about her own marriage, about the painful quarrels she had had with her husband over money and how she regretted not being able to say sorry to him before he died. She also told her about the many women she was now meeting in East London who seemed to have the same problems.

Gradually Mrs Crossman's defensive attitude melted away. The stern, hard face softened and she poured out to Annie her bitterness and fears. Finally she said she would like to take part in the work Annie was doing.

The following week, when Annie called on her again, Mrs Crossman remarked that her house had an extra bedroom and she would be pleased if Annie and her son and their friends would use the house in any way that would be helpful to them.

And so, in no time at all, the Crossman home became a busy headquarters for the whole East London orbit of Bill's work, constantly filled with people coming and going, and a place where Bill and his team could hold their daily planning meetings.

The old labour pioneers had trudged from house to house, ringing doorbells and talking with people to get their message across. It was also a natural way for Bill and Annie and their friends to meet people and tell them of the work they were doing.

They called on a home where there was a father, mother

and four children. The father had been out of work for a long time, and he came to the Jaegers' first big meeting in the Town Hall. When it was over he spoke to a couple of Bill's colleagues. It seemed he gambled a great deal, and never told his wife how much money he received on the dole, and so there was always a battle. He said, 'God wouldn't talk to me. I have been too vile to my family and would not work when I could.' Often he had taken the blankets and sheets off the bed to pawn them, to get money.

Bill's friends sat with him until almost midnight. They said, 'Are you willing to give God a chance to talk to you?' The man replied, 'Yes.' After some thought, his only clear idea was to go home and be honest with his wife.

Not knowing about this, a friend called at the home the next morning and was met by the man's wife who said, 'I can't think what has come over Ted. He came home from that meeting last night so different, and apologised to me for not being honest about money.'

* * * * *

A steady stream of new recruits kept turning up, asking Bill and Annie how they could help. One was Joy Wimbush, who was just at the start of a secretarial training:

'I walked into a gathering of others, also newly arrived, in the home of Edith Crossman in Stratford. Bill and Annie were staying there. I was taken to the home in Canning Town of Jock and Queenie Walker. It was late in the evening, and Jock and Queenie were in bed. But with true East London and Irish hospitality, Jock vacated his side of the bed and slept on the chairbed in his children's room, and I crept in beside Queenie.

'Jock was a tiler of roofs. One morning he and Queenie had a blazing row as he left for work. As the front door slammed behind him, Queenie shouted, "..and don't come back for dinner." I had never experienced such a situation before. All I could think was to go and fetch Annie. When

42

she came, the three of us talked in the kitchen. We ended by sitting quietly, taking heed of the still, small voice inside. At the end Queenie smiled and said to me, "Joy, go and find Jock, and tell him he can come back for dinner." Jock was at the top of a very high ladder to a roof. I had to shout the message up to him. I always remember his grin as he shouted back, "OK, Joy."

'As soon as Bill discovered I was learning to be a secretary he asked me to help with his letters. He paced up and down Mrs Crossman's front room, pouring out dictation. Very soon we both realised I was not up to the task, and Bill suggested we wait to repeat the experience until I had improved my skills.

'Every Sunday we all had lunch at *The Swan* with Bill and Annie. It was great fun, with Annie's laugh and Bill playing the piano.'

Bill and his team were by now holding meetings of between 700 and 1,000 all over East London. Then came opposition.

They awoke one morning to find that pavements in the centre of West Ham had been marked with chalk, 'Down with the Oxford Group, scared of the truth.'

Strong heckling began at all the meetings. Some would shout from the audience, trying to drown out what was being said from the platform. One night at a meeting of 300, when Annie and Bill were on the platform, flanked by other speakers, a crowd of about 35 communists started to sing 'The Red Flag' and to march down the sides of the hall to take over the platform.

Bill, realising what was happening, motioned to someone to go to the piano, got the audience on its feet and singing 'Bridgebuilders', conducting it himself. 'Bridgebuilders' out-sang 'The Red Flag'; the meeting ended and Bill led his colleagues down into the hall where they engaged in lively debate with the troublemakers, many of whom from that time on gave them support.

Undergraduates from Oxford and Cambridge, whose lives had been touched by the Oxford Group, began coming to the East End during their vacations. Bunny Austin, the tennis ace, was another who came to lend a hand, and through him Bill was able to meet the manager of West Ham Football Club, Charlie Paynter, who let the undergraduates use the club's changing rooms as temporary accommodation – blankets and camp-beds being brought in.

It was a strenuous life, beginning early in the morning and going on non-stop until after midnight. Meals were snatched when and where possible – not often at regular intervals. Yet the quality of Bill's commitment fired his colleagues with the same dedication. Such an aim brought a zest to living. There was much joking and leg-pulling between them all. Sometimes, around four in the afternoon, Bill would find a few free moments. At those times he loved to go to a small cafe, where he would order a plate of fish and chips, liberally add vinegar and then down it all with a large pot of tea.

Nor was the world of sport forgotten. Bill avidly followed the fortunes of all the football clubs, especially the two closest to his heart – Stockport County and West Ham United. He and his friends often managed to attend matches, joining the passionate crowds on the terraces urging on their favourites.

One day three of Bill's colleagues went to call in one of the tougher streets in the area. They knocked on one door, and when it was opened introduced themselves as from the Oxford Group. It turned out to be the home of Bill Rowell – head of The National Unemployment Workers Movement. Rowell was a powerful orator, and a militant Marxist.

The Rowells had had a three-month-old daughter who died in her mother's arms, not from ill-health so much as from lack of food. Many nights their children went to bed hungry because there was no money for food. Often in the evening the house was dark, as there was no penny for the

44

gas. Rowell's sense of outrage at the injustices all around led him to organise hunger marches, confrontations with police, and bitter strikes.

It was Bill Rowell's brother who opened the door to the men from the Oxford Group, and hearing the word 'Oxford', thought they were from the Oxford college to which Rowell had been writing, asking for the loan of blankets for a holiday planned for some of the unemployed in West Ham. He let the visitors in.

Something about the unexpected callers impressed Bill Rowell. 'Come around this evening, and we'll have a ding-dong,' he said to them.

The ding-dong ended up by Rowell, his wife Doris, and some of their colleagues being really bowled over by the stories they heard from the Oxford Group's work. They had never heard people talk so openly before. Tea was brought in on a tray every half hour, and the evening ended with arrangements to meet again.

The two Bills became close colleagues.

Frank Buchman took a keen interest in the developments in East London. He made several visits there himself and took tea in the homes of some of the trade unionists. He laid great stress on the winning and developing of 'the ordinary man'. It would appear that he realised Bill could develop and strengthen the labour and industrial side of his work.

In 1933 Buchman had met George Light, leader of the unemployed in Warwickshire. Light was a bitter man at the time, but became completely won over by Buchman.

In 1938 Bill was a guest at a luncheon Light gave for Buchman at the National Trade Union Club. Visiting London at the time was Harold Butler, Director-General of the International Labour Organisation (ILO). He also was one of the guests at the luncheon.

Buchman introduced Bill to Butler, and so to a world body which would become closely connected with Bill's life in future years. The ILO was the only remaining body left over from the original League of Nations. It had equal representation from government, management and labour.

* * * * *

Throughout 1938, Britain and Europe watched the advance of Fascism and Nazism under Mussolini and Hitler. Czechoslovakia was invaded. In everyone's thoughts was the dread of a second world war. Memories of the carnage of the First World War were still painful in most people's minds, the horrors, and in the end what seemed to some to have been a useless slaughter of millions of young men. Yet, only 20 years later, people wondered could there be peace? Did millions have to die again? How to contain Hitler?

A great debate took place throughout the year – should Britain and Europe rearm? There was a sense of foreboding in the air. Several influential observers, including Edward VIII, now Duke of Windsor, Charles Lindbergh, and Joseph Kennedy, the US Ambassador to London, had witnessed and assessed Hitler's war potential as almost unbeatable.

Buchman, deeply pondering the international situation like everyone else, had visited Sweden in the spring of 1938 and talked with some of the country's responsible people about the question of whether it would be peace or war. One man, Harry Blomberg, a Socialist writer, said to Buchman, 'The crisis is fundamentally a moral one.'

A short time later Buchman was staying in the Black Forest in Germany. Walking one day in the silence of the ancient woodland, Blomberg's phrase went round and round in his head. 'The real need is moral and spiritual rearmament' – the words ringing in his mind. 'The next great move in the world will be a movement of moral rearmament for all nations,' was his own extension of the original thought.

And so the Oxford Group became Moral Re-Armament. The phrase quickly caught on. The Queen of the

Netherlands in a radio broadcast called for moral re-armament. From London, King George VI's uncle, the Earl of Athlone, did the same.

The immediate question was how to launch it world-wide.

East London, the cradle of the British Labour movement, was the setting decided on, with East Ham Town Hall as the venue. On May 29, 1938, 3,000 poured into the hall; two overflow halls were used as well. Twenty-six mayors and chairmen of town councils were there, workers from the factories, the docks and railways, and also a large contingent of the unemployed.

Buchman was central on the platform, and the meeting was chaired by Bill, with Annie close by.

*   *   *   *   *

Throughout the Munich crisis and the launching in Britain of the new name of Moral Re-Armament (MRA), Buchman was in close touch with his Oxford Group colleagues in America. Many letters and cables were exchanged, and it was decided that this was the moment Buchman should return to America, to introduce the change of name and his broadened concept of MRA.

Early in 1939 Bill and Annie heard that Buchman would soon be going to America, taking quite a large group with him, probably for about three months.

Annie described what happened next:

'One day my son told me I had been invited to America.... I must admit that the thought of going to America really surprised me. For one thing, I was afraid of the ocean. I always had been. Another thing, I didn't know what the Americans would be like, especially the women, and I thought I might be afraid of them, too. It meant leaving my responsibilities and many friends in East London. I thought perhaps Bill was just teasing me, so I said, "Don't be silly."

'"Well," he said, "it isn't silly. They want you over

there to help them and to tell them about the work you have done in England."

'So I decided to go. I only had time to buy a hat. What woman, young or old, would ever think of travelling to America without a new hat!'

*   *   *   *   *

Buchman and a large party sailed to New York in March, 1939. Soon after arrival he confessed to being 'shocked' at the attitudes he found there. 'America has no sense of danger,' he said.

He felt there was a disturbing lack of understanding of the forces which threatened world peace. People did not want to face the facts, for example, about either Fascism or Communism. Deep in the country's thinking was George Washington's warning, 'to avoid entangling alliances'. At that time the US was still primarily made up of people who had fled Europe to escape from the constant wars.

Buchman felt deeply that America needed rousing, but how to do it?

Three mass meetings were planned, and took place within three months of each other. The first was in Madison Square Gardens, New York, where 12,000 people packed the hall. The second was in Constitution Hall in Washington, DC. Then across the country to the West Coast, to California and the Hollywood Bowl, where the campaign culminated in a massive meeting of 30,000 people, and 10,000 turned away, unable to get in, as Buchman's world force addressed the vast audience.

The press coverage of these meetings was thorough and helpful in bringing Moral Re-Armament to the attention not only of America but many other parts of the world.

In August, 1939, came the announcement of the Nazi-Communist pact. It was clear enough that Hitler was a threat to world peace, but the left-wing, pro-Communist press in America, along with the considerable support

Communism had in the States, were forced to do a quick reversal of propaganda, since Hitler had suddenly become an ally. Ordinary people ended up very confused about what to believe.

On September 3, 1939, came the invasion of Poland by Germany, and England declared war.

Even Roosevelt at that time was cautious about showing support for Britain's policies. Possibly, in his heart, he wanted to, but the reality of politics prevented him from saying so publicly – he was up for election on a platform that supported peace.

Buchman was well before his time in understanding the aims that Communists under Stalin had in mind. And though, after the attack on Poland, the US began to accept that Hitler's war could become a threat even to America, Buchman believed that America had little general understanding of the ideological forces at work.

He felt the need of someone who could support and strengthen the impact and leadership of MRA in the US. And so he cabled Bill in London, asking him to consider coming to America to do this – and if possible to bring Bill Rowell with him. Bunny Austin received a similar invitation.

All three men had to seek, and were given, special permission to travel by the Ministry of Labour, the Ministry of Information and the Foreign Office, and in December, 1939, they set sail for New York, in a liner blacked out against submarine attack.

IV

America – a wartime challenge

Arriving in New York Bill found himself in a different world. Bright lights, plenty of food, big cars; life continuing as if no war was on.

He was now 27 years old. Annie was on the west coast of America.

Buchman received the three travellers and they were quickly included in a series of dates in New York, meeting a great variety of people from society families to the President of the inner-city Borough of Queens. There was a strong, active Oxford Group work in New York City at that time, a great deal of it emanating from Calvary Church in Gramercy Park, where Samuel Shoemaker was the rector.

It was not long before Bill began to realise that some of the Americans he was meeting were unhappy about the change of the name of the Oxford Group to Moral Re-Armament. This was most noticeable among those connected with the thriving Calvary Church parish.

The emphasis on personal change as the main goal of the Oxford Group had been very successful, resulting in thousands of changed lives across the world. Some people felt a wrong turning was being taken, in the attempt to broaden the Oxford Group's original concept through Moral Re-Armament, and to relate personal change to the political, social and national field.

But some months later Bill was able to bring reconciliation among certain of the protagonists in the argument. As Buchman said, 'Moral and spiritual re-armament is the programme of the Oxford Group', and it was a unifying concept.

*　　*　　*　　*　　*

However, Bill's prime task was to address the thinking of people in American industry, broadening their understanding of the ideological issues across the world.

One man Bill met in those busy early weeks in America was someone he was to work closely with for the next seven years. Charles Haines was from a distinguished Philadelphia Quaker family connected with the steel industry, owning a plant called Lukens Steel. He knew the industry from the bottom up, having started work in the open hearth as a young man. He was a tall, rather dashing figure, and had met the Oxford Group at Princeton in the twenties.

Charles Haines introduced Bill to a red-headed man of Bill's own age. Warner Clark, like Haines, had the Philadelphia Quaker background which had helped give him a social conscience. He was always looking for ways to make life more tolerable for those caught in the poverty trap. He had spent a year in the desolate coalmining area of Ohio, seeking to make improvements to the wretched shacks where the miners tried to raise their families. In 1936 he met the Oxford Group, and decided its approach to problems went deeper than housing improvements, necessary as they were.

In New York one day, in connection with the Oxford Group, Warner Clark met an official of the Steelworkers' union, John Ramsay, and began making visits to the great steel plant at Bethlehem, Pennsylvania, where Ramsay worked, trying to explain the new ideas he had come to believe in. But, until Bill Jaeger's arrival, there had not been many other contacts with American unions. There was no real nationwide plan to inform and enlist the important force that labour represented. Haines and Clark quickly realised that through Bill and his colleagues they had a chance to open up a whole new field.

They were soon joined by a young shipyard worker from the Clyde, Duncan Corcoran. A fiery Scot, he had come to America with a group of 12 others from Scotland to speak at the mass meetings arranged by Buchman some months earlier. He had known the degradation and frustration of unemployment, and the resulting despair and bitterness, and was a passionate speaker. He was now giving his full time to the work of MRA.

Duncan was to become Bill Jaeger's inseparable colleague during the next years. They were of a similar height and stocky shape, both had a natural warmth and outgoing quality that made friends easily, both spoke with fire and conviction at meetings, and both revelled in the task they had undertaken.

With the group they now had, Haines and Clark made arrangements to travel across the country, meeting representatives of labour, management and civic life wherever they could. They knew they had convincing speakers who could address both sides of the industrial divide, creating bridges from one person to another.

Feb 20, 1940. Bill to Annie:
'Last Sunday night in Baltimore I spoke at a dinner of 110 of the principal businessmen and doctors, headmasters, lawyers. It was broadcast on the radio. There was a luncheon meeting of 30 men the following day. I stayed in the home of a Mr and Mrs Dorsey. We also met the president of the Steelworkers and the Governor of the State. The mayor came to breakfast. We discovered Senator Taft, a Republican candidate for the Presidency, was staying in our hotel, so we went to see him. I could do with more hours in the day.'

An important date was laid on for the end of February

in Columbus, Ohio, when the United Mineworkers were holding their annual convention.

Haines' plan was for Bill, Duncan and Bill Rowell to meet one of the most famous people in the United States – the President of the United Mineworkers. John L Lewis was a broad, solid figure, with a mane of thick grey hair and bushy eyebrows. He was a volcano of a man, an eloquent speaker. He had become Public Enemy No 1 to many in American management. Haines, no stranger to these conventions, took his three British friends onto the platform of the hall and introduced them to Lewis, who received them warmly and invited them to take seats on the platform as distinguished visitors from overseas.

It was the period of the Nazi-Communist pact in the early part of the war. Bill found himself profoundly shaken to see, from his vantage point on the platform, that all around the walls of the auditorium were large placards saying 'Down with England and the War of British Imperialism'. Even more disturbing was the sight of a large red flag emblazoned with the hammer and sickle being lowered behind the dais when Lewis, apparently unaware of the backdrop he was being given, got up to speak.

'This taking over of the Mineworkers' convention was the first time I really began to understand the ideological struggle going on in American labour,' Bill said. 'It opened my eyes and prepared me for what I would find commonplace in the country in the next six years.'

It was, Bill realised, one of the many tactics being used by the Communists to keep America confused, and unwilling to give any aid to Britain or Europe.

Many American unions contained Communist and non-Communist (Socialist) factions, constantly at war with each other for control. As he moved from city to city, Bill began to absorb and understand the history of the American labour movement. In these travels he developed a habit that would stay with him for the next 50 years: while visiting any office giving free printed information about its particular field, Bill would help himself to pamphlets, leaflets and magazines on display, stuffing them into his pockets or briefcase. This printed matter took up much more room in his suitcases than his clothes, which had to be packed in, around or underneath them.

Apart from the Mineworkers there were two other large groups: the craft unions, called the American Federation of Labor (AFL), and the industrial unions, called the Congress of International Organisations (CIO).

Haines took Bill and Duncan (Bill Rowell having returned to Britain and the army by this time) to meet Philip Murray, president of the United Steelworkers Union, and vice-president of the CIO nationally. Murray was born in Scotland, his family emigrating to America in 1902. At 16 he went to work for the Keystone Coal and Coke Co.

A tall, grey-haired figure with a deceptively benign appearance, Murray responded immediately to his British visitors as they told him how they wanted to support American labour. He said, 'The best national defence America can have is good morale among the people, and any movement that does this deserves our strong support.'

He later gave Haines the name of a man he would like them to meet, saying 'John Riffe is my best organiser, but he needs help.' It seemed what he needed help with was too much poker playing, too much whisky, and a subsequent tendency to get into brawls. Murray told Bill and Duncan that his door would always be open to them.

Bill, Duncan and Charles finally completed the 3,000-mile journey across America, arriving in San Francisco in April, and at last Bill met up with his mother.

He was glad to discover that she was very much at home in America. 'The tall women with loud voices', as she had once described them while still in England, no longer frightened her. She took them on in her exceptional way of friendship, just as she had done in East London, and they responded in kind.

Soon after arriving in San Francisco, Charles Haines

followed Philip Murray's suggestion, and got on the phone to the office of John Riffe. At that time Riffe was West Coast director of the Steelworkers' Organising Committee, a pioneer union among the giant industrial unions. A luncheon date was suggested by Haines, which Riffe was quick to accept when he heard that Murray had recommended the meeting.

Riffe, a mountain of a man, clearly no stranger to trouble and confrontation, was not hard to identify in the hotel lobby. He brought along a fellow steelworker, Jim Thimmes. To begin with the two union men were slightly wary, but were soon disarmed by the combination of friendliness and candour displayed by their hosts.

At the beginning of the lunch they asked Riffe about his own early life. He had gone down the mines at 14, which meant there had been little time for any schooling. His life had been one long slog, through ups and downs, to the point where he now was – convinced that the steelworkers needed to be organised and united to fight for their rights.

'I carried all my life a deep bitterness and hatred against employers,' Riffe told them. His burning passion for justice had made him 'the roughest, toughest man in the steelworkers'.

The two men listened as Bill, Duncan and Charles began to explain the work they were engaged in, 'how to build a better society for everybody'. Bill said to them, 'Marx's slogan, "Workers of the world, unite!" may have been relevant to the nineteenth century, but in the twentieth, millions need a bigger idea: "Workers, unite the world!"'

They felt an immediate rapport with Duncan Corcoran, and the struggles he had gone through as an unemployed shipyard worker.

As for Charles Haines, a management man who ordinarily would have been suspect, the steelmen found a man who understood the need for the unions to organise, and who made it clear that selfish management must change. For Haines, people came before profit – and such a man could be trusted.

The two steelworkers had never heard anything like it before. They went away with plans to meet again, and soon.

Bill told his mother about the luncheon, and on learning that a Steelworkers' convention was shortly to be held in San Francisco, he asked her if she could find a way to meet Mrs Riffe, who would be in town.

He found out the name of their hotel, and so Annie and a friend, June Lee, bought some flowers on a street corner, went to the hotel lobby phone, and called up Mrs Riffe's room. Annie introduced herself as coming from England, and asked if she could come up to meet Mrs Riffe.

Mrs Riffe's face registered some suspicion when she opened the door, but at the sight of the small white-haired lady holding out a bunch of flowers, she quickly welcomed the visitors in.

In the next hour Annie and June Lee learned that she was the second Mrs John Riffe, and that John was her second husband. Family life had grown complicated, but the main problems seemed to be John's wayward ways.

Rose Riffe became a friend of Annie's that afternoon, and said she would really like to help her husband. It dawned on her that her nagging and suspicions might also be part of the problem at home.

The next step was an invitation to the Riffes and two other steelworkers' organisers and their wives to attend an MRA 'Round Table' conference in Brookdale, California. Charles Haines told them that there they would meet others in labour and management, seeking ways to answer industrial strife.

The Riffes and their friends went along, though John took the precaution of putting a case of whisky in the car.

The whisky was never used. He found himself meeting employers like Charles Haines, men with the same kind of open attitude to labour's problems. He met Frank Buchman also, who told him that MRA meant change –

starting with oneself. John did not feel he needed to change.

'That's fine, that's fine,' Buchman responded. 'Maybe there's someone else you'd like to see different.'

Before the year's end Riffe said, 'By applying the principle of honesty, I have been able to achieve more for my union in three months than in the past three years.'

Through the next years Riffe made sincere efforts to apply the principles of MRA into his organising work. The habits of a lifetime were not easy to break, and his opponents knew they could easily goad him into losing his temper. In exasperation John still sometimes found the whisky bottle was the fastest escape route, and that using his fists was the quickest way to settle an argument.

There were ups and downs for Rose, as her feelings continued to get the better of her at times, in spite of resolutions to try and stop being suspicious and blaming John.

There was one really positive advance in their home life, when they decided to collect all the children from their respective marriages under one roof, together with their youngest daughter, Joanna. The lively household also included Rose's mother, Grandma Stein.

Making contact with John Riffe had been a priority for Bill after arriving in California with Haines and his party, and they remained friends for the rest of John Riffe's life.

V

A nationwide response

The spectacular meeting held in the Hollywood Bowl just before war broke out in 1939 had resulted in thousands of people up and down the West coast of America wanting to know more about Moral Re-Armament.

In California, several more men and women joined up with Bill, creating a group who for the next six years would make it their aim to bring a uniting spirit into the American unions. There were four more Scots who joined them: Blyth Ramsay and Adam McLean from the Clyde, Tom Gillespie, a clerk, and Stuart Smith, a champion chess player and brilliant Glasgow University scholar. Along with Corcoran, these young men had been part of the delegation of 12 who had come in 1939, with kilts and bagpipes, to take part in the mass demonstrations launched in that year, and they stayed on in America to be involved in the detailed, personal work being undertaken by Buchman.

Duncan Corcoran described how they operated:

'Bill's quality as a team builder became very apparent. He included people in whatever he was doing, encouraged them and took them to meet union leaders and to union meetings. It was a new world for many. His passionate commitment was a driving force in the labour team.

'He always believed in "having the facts", and was not satisfied until he got the picture clear.

'As we moved into the different cities of America, he

developed a very effective method of working. On arrival he would get hold of the local telephone book and make a dozen copies of the yellow page section which listed all the trade unions, their addresses, and their officials. He would tick off about six homes on each sheet and give each of his team a different list, asking us to call on them and report back in a few days' time. After a week of this we would have contacted the top union officials in a town. As this work went on week after week, month after month, year after year, a highly experienced group was formed with contacts throughout the nation.'

Annie had occasional need for a driver, to take her to meet the civic and union wives she was caring for. In California it was not possible simply to walk from place to place, as she had done in London. To help her, two young Californian women became part of the Jaeger team at that time. June Lee, who had accompanied Annie to meet Rose Riffe, was one, and Polly Ann Eastman, daughter of the President of the Los Angeles Chamber of Commerce, was the other. Recently graduated from college, Polly Ann found herself intrigued by the chance that working with Bill and Annie offered, of getting to know people in union circles.

Like Bill, Annie was extremely sensitive to what anyone she had contact with might be feeling. A strong friendship developed between June and Annie, Annie sensing a certain sadness in the younger woman. Bit by bit Annie drew her out. June had been married for ten years but was now divorced, her husband married to someone else. June was quite clear that the break-up was all her husband's fault.

At one point Annie said, 'If you were married for ten years, there must be *something* you need to put right with your husband.'

There was indeed. The remark cast a whole new light on the situation, and was a turning point in June's life. She ended up going to see her former husband, and his new

60

wife, with the result that a healing took place between the three of them.

* * * * *

As Americans read in their press the news of Hitler's march across Europe, the mood in the United States began to change. By 1941 not many still felt that it was merely a war of British imperialism. Norway, Denmark, Holland and France were all occupied. Would England be next?

In the face of this disturbing daily news, Buchman decided to gather together his most trusted colleagues, to find what he described as deeper spiritual roots. Mass meetings were fine, and of great benefit, but without the most fundamental and personal commitment, their fruit would perish. Bill and Annie were among the group that gathered with Buchman in California.

They were all together for some three months, and out of that time a deeper honesty and trust was born between the men and women in whom Buchman invested so much hope. And, almost incidentally, a new medium to address the needs and thinking of the country also came to birth. It took the form of a patriotic musical revue called *You Can Defend America*. It had catchy songs and a series of sketches and scenes. The theme was 'sound homes, team-work in industry, a united nation'. A handbook had been written, to elaborate on these three points.

About 200 people were involved in putting on the show and travelling with it: about 50 were in the cast, some as lead players and some as extras. There was a back-stage group, handling the lighting, stage scenery, costumes. Some of these were also on the stage during performances. About 50 others came along to make the forward preparations to receive the group and provide transport.

The revue opened in Carson City, Nevada, and had an immediate impact on the thinking of the audience. Then on to Reno, and the same warm reception.

There was a thorough distribution of the handbook

across the country. Its red, white and blue cover touched a strong note of patriotism.

On the East coast, civilian Defence Committees were being set up to prepare local communities for America's possible intervention in the war. Some Defence Committees were sent the handbook, and began issuing invitations to have the revue brought to their cities. An Eastern première was to take place in Bridgeport, Connecticut, at the invitation of the Bridgeport Brass Company.

Bill travelled east from California to join up with the show, in order to inform the union officials in different cities on the schedule, and ensuring that their membership received tickets.

The day Bill arrived in Connecticut from California the whole company with the revue were invited for a post-rehearsal meal by one of the local families. Long trestle tables had been set up under the trees in the garden, and a buffet supper laid out.

It was a lovely warm summer evening. Bill helped himself, and then took his seat at one of the tables. Part way through his meal, a young woman from the cast squeezed herself into an empty space next to him and dug into her meal. He glanced at her, seeing a mass of curly brown hair and bright brown eyes. She nodded and smiled in greeting, but said nothing.

Her proximity brought on him an attack of shyness, and finishing his meal as quickly as he could he got up and left the table.

How surprised and even startled Bill would have been if someone had told him that this was the girl he would marry.

*   *   *   *   *

As Bill and his colleagues moved around the country with the revue, calling on the local unions, both CIO and AFL, in every city and town they visited, the fact that the top men of the national unions had openly endorsed the work of Moral Re-Armament immediately gained the interest of local union presidents and secretaries.

The leaders of America's great unions had firsthand knowledge of the revue and handbook. William Green, President of the American Federation of Labor, said, 'I hope *You Can Defend America* will be in the hands of every union man in the country. It will help towards that teamwork in industry which is essential if our armed forces are to have the backing they deserve.'

Philip Murray, President of the Congress of International Organisations, gave his own assessment. '*You Can Defend America* brings us all back to fundamentals. It charts in brief, compelling outline the practical programme for home, industry and nation.'

Throughout the war a network of union men and women was brought into being, who endorsed and to varying extents carried into practice the principle of re-placing suspicion with trust. In dealings with management, as well as disruptive factions in the unions themselves, they began to have dialogue where there had been sit-downs and strikes, and perhaps even more basically, many real-ised how to undergird and strengthen their union work with a sound home life.

Wherever Bill and his team had set out to bring a new spirit into labour and industry, there were no strings attached. Bill had always had the genuine desire to listen to people and find out what life was like. He always sought for a depth of understanding that went beyond making friends on a superficial level, so that the real needs in peo-ple could be addressed.

It could all start with a knock at the door, a date pre-arranged on the telephone, or after meeting up at a labour convention.

Even though Bill worked primarily with his labour group during the war years, he also formed warm friend-ships simultaneously with some of Buchman's American colleagues working in quite different fields. Among them

63

were three Princeton men: Ray Purdy, who had returned to Princeton from Wall Street, Kenaston Twitchell, son-in-law of a US Senator, and who had been one of Buchman's closest colleagues in Oxford in the 1930s, and Scoville Wishard who also had worked with Buchman from the earliest years. Another was John Roots, son of Bishop Roots of Hankow. John was a journalist, and because of his upbringing in China he retained many close ties and friendships with that country for the rest of his life.

These men, along with Charles Haines, gave constant support to Bill in the pioneering work he was doing in their country. And Bill also made many friends among the management of American industry. He never cut himself off from any section of society, and his own working class background provided him with a bridge to everyone he met.

For 18 months Bill and Annie and their friends travelled up and down the east coast of America, from Maine to Florida. Bill organised and set in operation the system he had first used in East London; a card index was set up as well as lists drawn up of the labour men and their wives. In addition to keeping up these records, Bill and Duncan were constantly writing letters to the people they met.

The sheer volume of the paperwork increased daily, and by the time they reached Florida in the winter of 1940 the need for more secretarial help had become urgent.

Bill discovered from Warner Clark that his sister Clara, who was in the revue and helped with the costumes, was also a trained secretary. He and Duncan decided to offer her an invitation to join them and Warner and give them a hand.

It was Clara Clark – 'Click' as she was known by everyone – who had sat down next to Bill at the open-air meal in Connecticut. She had left an impression on him that evening, an impression carefully filed away at the back of his mind. He watched her singing in the chorus of the

7 Frank Buchman

8 Annie Jaeger

9 Annie and Bill Jaeger sing 'Bridgebuilders' with Frank Buchman and friends at *The King's Head*, East London

10 & 11 San Francisco, USA. Bill Jaeger and Duncan Corcoran (right) came here in April, 1940, at the request of Philip Murray, National President of the United Steelworkers' Union. He asked them to see his West Coast organiser, John Riffe. 'He is my best organiser, but he needs help.'

12 Philip Murray, National President, United Steelworkers of America

13 John Riffe of the Steelworkers' Union, with his wife Rose and their daughter Joanna

revue night after night, and liked what he saw.

On the surface she did not seem a particularly likely candidate to work in the field of labour unions; she had moved in New York literary circles, and there was some talk about her 'past'. She was evidently rather an unconventional character, but the need for help was great.

Bill and Duncan presented their case to Warner's sister. At first she explained that she was busy in the show, and also helping with the costumes. She had heard from another friend that Bill made you work very hard.

'But you do also type, don't you?' they persisted.

She admitted that she did.

Striking while the iron was hot, they invited her to go with them to visit the local Brewery Workers' Union, where they were headed to issue invitations for the evening show and address some of the delegates to a convention. She accepted.

And from that day I was swept into the fast-moving life of Bill's group.

VI

Detroit and Philadelphia

1941-42

Americans lived daily into reports of the war in Europe, and could see clearly enough that nothing must be allowed to stop the flow of arms from the factories, which were essential for the fighting forces in Europe. But American unions were riddled with strife. First of all there was distrust and even hatred of management. Then the unions had their own warring factions, between the socialists and communists. Then a walkout could be caused, for example by the presence of black workers.

The factories were constantly faced with the threat of walkouts and strikes arising from any or all these issues. It gave impetus and urgency to what Bill and those of us working with him were doing.

Then on Sunday morning, December 6, 1941, every radio in the land broadcast news of the Japanese attack on Pearl Harbour. The mood in the country changed immediately.

For the next few months *You Can Defend America*, now called a wartime revue, was in even more demand from the heads of the Civic Defence Committees.

In the spring of 1942 the show headed for Detroit, where it opened in the 5,000-seat Civic Auditorium. Bill arrived in the city very keen to get going, already knowing something of Detroit's labour history, so much of which centred around the famous UAW – United Automobile Workers' Union.

Of all the great cities of America, Detroit was the most challenging, and perhaps at this point in history one of the most important. It had sprung into being because of the motor car, and grew from a small village beside the Great Lakes, to a city of over two million. There were the huge car plants – Ford, Chrysler, General Motors – pioneered largely by Henry Ford and his $5 a day wage, and the assembly line.

It was a hard city, a tough city, and with many foreign workers. Hamtramck, for instance, a municipality entirely surrounded by Detroit and home of the main Dodge factory, boasted more Polish inhabitants than Warsaw.

The giant plants made millions for their owners. Then began the bloody battle to unionise the workers. Long picket lines formed outside the factory gates as labour fought for a living wage against powerful management. Some employers hired 'goons' with batons and guns to prevent the union forming. But gradually labour won through, and the UAW was born. Bill met many leaders of the UAW – R J Thomas, Richard Frankenstein, and the Reuther brothers, Walter, Victor and Roy – all of them major figures in American industry.

Now after the shock of Pearl Harbour, all these vast factories had been converted to producing weapons of war, the city gaining the label, 'The Arsenal of Democracy'.

Before *You Can Defend America* opened, hundreds of union offices were visited by Bill and his group, to inform the members about the show. At the Briggs Body plant, for instance, a group of us stood on a tall platform and addressed the workers through a bull horn as they gathered outside the plant in the summer sunshine in their lunch hour.

68

As usual, the show was packed out, and played every night for a week, by the end of which time Bill had made some valuable acquaintances who would become friends and colleagues.

*   *   *   *   *

By the autumn of 1942 the draft was getting well under way and Bill was summoned to go before the board in New York City, which had been his port of entry. At no point had the British authorities requested his return for military service, and his passport was marked 'clergyman', which should have exempted him. In addition he had a letter of support for his work from the secretary of the Baptist Church in England.

Bill's interview turned out to be quite unpleasant. The examining board, which contained a left-wing faction, took a negative view of Moral Re-Armament. Bill happened to know that the board had already exempted several well-known Communist activists, but they brushed aside his attempts to explain the work he was doing in the United States.

The chairman said to Bill, 'We have read your credentials, Mr Jaeger, and there really is no room for the Holy Spirit today.'

He was put in category 1A, which meant he was to be drafted into the armed services immediately.

However, the Selective Service Board in Washington had given its full support to the work MRA was doing for industry and in the factories. The Draft Board was overruled, with President Roosevelt placing his stamp of agreement on the document, and Bill was told to continue as before.

Except for a few men who on health grounds were classed category 4F (unfit for military service), all other MRA full-time workers in America now went into the armed forces. It was no longer possible or practical to mount the revue, and those remaining divided up to continue their programme in the factories as best they could. Most went to the west coast, where the aeronautical industry was centred. A handful settled in to work in Detroit, Bill among them.

*   *   *   *   *

Through all these months Annie had continued to travel with the show, using the opportunity to get to know and befriend the wives of the union men Bill met in all the different cities. In the spring of 1942 Rosamund Lombard, a member of the cast of the revue, began to take Annie under her wing. The strenuous travel and constantly meeting new people was hard enough for the younger people, but Annie was in her 60s.

Then, when they arrived in Detroit, Annie confessed to Rosamund that she really felt quite unwell. Rosamund immediately arranged for Annie to see a doctor, who then sent her for tests. The tests showed that she had cancer.

Mr and Mrs Henry Ford had seen *You Can Defend America* and Annie had been introduced to Mrs Ford. Through mutual friends, word reached Mrs Ford about Annie's condition. She arranged at once for her to be given a room in the city's Henry Ford Hospital and put under the care of specialists.

It was obvious now that Bill would stay on in Detroit, but he would want a team to work with.

He consulted with friends, and ended up with a group of six including himself. There were June Lee and myself for secretarial work, Tom Gillespie who wrote a weekly column for the many labour papers who wanted news of MRA's outreach, George Vondermuhll, a Princeton man who had worked in a Massachusetts textile mill, at the ILO in Geneva, and on *Business Week* magazine, and Rosamund, who was so close to his mother.

Bill was invited to stay in the home of the Sanger family in Grosse Pointe, an area some 20 miles east of downtown Detroit, on the shores of Lake St Claire.

Henry Sanger was Henry Ford's banker. His wife Margaret was a warmhearted, motherly woman, who had known Buchman and his team for many years. She not only offered to have Bill to stay, but said he could set up an office in the basement games room. The billiard table was in the middle of the room, and Mrs Sanger brought in card-tables and chairs for us to use as office desks.

Bill settled down with this small group to continue the morale-building work in the city. He worked us hard. The point now was to keep up the contacts with those men and women, primarily in the unions, who had shown interest, and who were already putting into practice new ways of dealing with divisions and strife.

We met each morning at nine, having spent time talking with our respective hostesses over breakfast. We would pool our experiences of the day before, and any thoughts we might have about how things had gone, and then Bill would take over.

He would talk passionately to us about the need to study and read, to know the history and background of situations, to understand why certain developments were taking place. Yet he cautioned us about the need to read with discernment. 'Don't just blindly accept everything you read,' he would say. What was the political background or motivation of those who held forth, for instance? Bill knew, and was able to reach objective conclusions because of his extensive reading and his accumulated understanding of the issues in the world.

'Newspapers, big and small, dailies, weeklies, conservative, socialist, Trotskyite, Communist, of every kind and orientation; they were always there, under Bill's arm or under his bed, ready to be devoured with incredible speed whenever he had a moment to get at them. They were the source of much of his wide range of standard and unusual information,' as George Vondermuhll described it.

What I found most helpful in Bill's thinking and approach was that it took me way out beyond what had often been a losing struggle to be 'good' for its own sake, into an understanding of the war of ideas – the thinking that controlled people's minds and so determined the destiny of us all.

We were all kept very busy. The card index was used, as usual, but now Bill also required lists to be typed up. Discussions, planning, the dictation, the typing would go on through the morning. Then he went off to the hospital – an hour's drive away – to see Annie, then some visiting of homes, then a bite to eat, then more visiting, then, quite late at night a hot drink and a snack, sitting on a stool at a counter at one of the many all-night diners, and finally home to bed.

It happened gradually, my falling in love with Bill, though even before I met him, I had had a curiosity about him. I had heard stories about him from some of my friends.

I had been in love many times before, but I had never met anyone like Bill. I found him absolutely unique. He didn't fit into any known category. We saw each other every day, and at close quarters, week after week, and month after month, and then one day I just knew. When Bill was in the room, for me the whole atmosphere came alive.

I found it refreshing the way he cut through red tape, or ignored it. Many times I heard him say, 'I am not orthodox.' Perhaps I could say the same about myself. Bill plunged to the heart of the matter when he was discussing a problem. And if someone suggested that something was 'too difficult', Bill reacted strongly. That kind of attitude would make him at least as annoyed, if not angry, as anything else anyone could say. I sensed in him an indomitable will, backed by his faith that God would find a way if one just gave it a go.

*   *   *   *   *

72

In those 18 months in Detroit Bill never missed a day in going to see Annie in hospital. She had several operations after the first major one. Mrs Ford was one of the many visitors who came to see her, and her room was often full of nurses and staff who liked to drop in on her. She took such an interest in them all, as individuals and also in their families. She wrote letters daily, many to the young men from the revue who were in the armed services. Their photographs in uniform were framed and placed around the hospital room, where she could look at them.

It was impressive to notice the lack of self-pity and self-concern between mother and son. There was plenty of banter and affectionate joking. If by any chance someone was down, or there was a shadow in the atmosphere, Annie would sense it and delicately help to track down the root cause. And of course, for me at any rate, admitting the real cause would bring release and freedom. With me, it was so often jealousy. After becoming serious about Bill, I was tempted to wonder if I had any rivals.

* * * * *

Bill left Detroit twice during those months, to visit his colleagues on the west coast. Blyth Ramsay, whom he especially wanted to see, was billeted in the home of the Holland family in Pasadena, California. Leland, the older son, was a shop steward at Lockheeds, one of the main factories turning out P38 fighter planes. Leland got to know Dale Reed, president of Aeronautical Industrial Lodge no. 727, Industrial Association of Machinists, AFL, which had 70,000 members. Reed felt that the *You Can Defend America* handbook would be helpful in building morale in the huge factory, where the usual slowdowns often happened. The top management agreed with him, with the result that 40,000 copies of the handbook were distributed through the plant. A short time later the management requested a further 30,000 copies.

Dale Reed said later, 'These men have perfected a

victory revue which is the most outstanding weapon of its kind I know for rousing men to increased efforts on behalf of the country.

'The revue is only an introduction, however, to the real work of these fellows, which is going on day and night in personal contact with war workers. Through these personal contacts they are bringing the means of production on the human side as surely as steel is necessary on the material side. These men have achieved a unique effectiveness in harmonising labour-management relationships and factional differences within labour.

'There are planes on the fighting fronts today that would not be there but for the enthusiasm and unselfish leadership the MRA workers have brought into the ranks of labour.'

At the Boeing plant in Seattle, where the 'Flying Fortresses' were produced, the union leader, Gary Cotton, said, 'In my work as president of the Boeing Union, I have been greatly helped by the Moral Re-Armament workers... they possess the rare ability to bring a change in cantankerous human nature, which releases and steps up productive power.'

In the spring of 1943 Senator Harry Truman, who became US President after Roosevelt's death, said, 'I have noticed that the chief difficulty of our war programme of industry is usually the human factor. Suspicions, rivalries, apathy and greed lie behind most bottlenecks. Any answer to these problems is of first importance to the war effort... these problems, to which the Moral Re-Armament programme is finding an effective solution, are the most urgent in our whole production picture.'

*   *   *   *   *

Shipbuilding and the shipyards was an area of industry equally as important as the aircraft factories for the war effort. At an MRA summer conference held in Michigan in 1943 Bill got to know Bill Schaffer, the president of the

74

17,000-strong shipyard workers' union at Cramps Shipyard in Philadelphia.

Schaffer had been invited to the conference by the vice-president of the company, who was hoping they both could find an answer to the many disputes and rivalries which were raging in the yard.

Bill brought a group of us up with him from Detroit to attend the conference. He recognised that Bill Schaffer was a key man in a key industry, but beset by all manner of difficulties.

His wife, Irene, was nicknamed Dynamite by John L Lewis, the president of the United Mineworkers, when he met her on the picket lines. Politically motivated elements in the union who wanted to take control were using blackmail to keep Schaffer quiet. They made regular anonymous telephone calls to Dynamite, telling her that her husband had been seen out the night before with a redhead.

By the time the couple arrived at the Michigan conference they were planning a divorce, after ten years of marriage and two small children.

Some of us got to know Dynamite, and had many long talks with her and her husband. We hit it off as friends. By the end of the conference Bill and Dynamite Schaffer said perhaps they would not divorce after all, and promised to keep in close touch with us.

*   *   *   *   *

Annic's illness progressed to the point where the specialists suggested she be moved to a place where she could be cared for and surrounded by friends, as they could do no more for her. My parents invited her to our home in Philadelphia, where she and Bill were at the heart of all that we were doing.

We made regular visits to the Schaffer home on the outskirts of the city, fulfilling our promise to keep in touch. Bit by bit Bill and Dynamite opened up to us about their problems. It seemed gambling on the horses was part of

75

the real trouble. Schaffer was afraid to tell his wife the truth, but one day he finally did so. Dynamite's first reaction was to want to hit him, but then she smiled, and accepted his apology. As Schaffer himself expressed it later, 'My problems were slow horses and fast women.'

Their marriage became completely remade. Schaffer followed Bill Jaeger's example, and built a team to work with him, and a new spirit came into the shipyard.

Birch Taylor, vice-president of the company, said in a public statement: 'The programme of *You Can Defend America* dramatises as nothing else does the philosophy of harmonious industrial relations .... Particular credit in this regard should be given to a small group of Britishers ... who have gained the respect and gratitude of employees and employers alike in many of our most vital war industries. I regard the work of these men and their American colleagues as a mainstay of the nation's war production drive. It is my considered opinion that their work in industry has already been worth a sizeable task force to the navy.'

*   *   *   *   *

Annie lived four more months, with a constant stream of visitors, both old and new friends.

We all knew how she loved the old gospel hymns, and throughout the last 48 hours many of them were sung to her. Bill himself hardly left her room, standing by her bed and holding her hand, speaking to her.

After she died Bill had over 500 letters from people whose family life became united through meeting Annie.

Frank Buchman wrote, 'She lived the miracle of being poor, yet making many rich; of having nothing, yet possessing all things.'

*   *   *   *   *

After his mother's funeral Bill was invited by Buchman,

76

who had suffered a stroke in 1942 and who was wintering in Florida, to join him and the group with him there. Bill travelled down by train, sporting his winter overcoat. He was affectionately welcomed by many old friends who were working in the community along with Buchman. They urged Bill to relax and rest; to go to the beach and sun himself.

Beach life was something quite unknown to Bill. He had never gone swimming in his life. Much to the amusement of his friends, he sat all day on the beach, in his overcoat, in glorious sunshine, reading as many newspapers as he could get his hands on.

But after Annie's death and Bill's departure our Germantown home seemed very quiet. My mother said of him, 'Heart, brain and character make him a peer among men.' Even though he never said so, it had become quite clear to me that Bill cared for me.

* * * * *

After his holiday in Florida Bill returned to Philadelphia, to continue his support of Bill Schaffer.

Also, and of particular interest to Bill, was the fact that the International Labour Organisation was about to hold its 26th annual conference in Philadelphia. During the war, the ILO had moved from Geneva to Montreal, and this meeting in Philadelphia was to be a special reunion time.

Bill with his friends moved around the conference, meeting the delegates. Len Allen, the broadcaster known as 'The Voice of China' from his work in Chungking some years earlier, was also in Philadelphia and introduced Bill to the Workers' delegate to the ILO from China. He was Mr Zhu Xuefan, founder of the Chinese trade unions in Shanghai.

Bill and Len Allen arranged for Mr Zhu Xuefan to visit some American homes, and to meet people whom he might perhaps ordinarily not have come into contact with. One was the editor of *The Progressive Labour World*, a paper which carried news of the work of MRA every week in its columns.

Bill and Zhu Xuefan became firm friends, as they met and talked on a number of occasions in the course of that conference in Philadelphia. Zhu Xuefan had been a postman in Shanghai, and later became President of the Postmen's Union of China.

A short while after this Buchman took his group, including Bill, to San Francisco in 1945, to attend the opening ceremonies of the United Nations. Zhu Xuefan was also there, and Bill and he met again. Bill introduced his Chinese friend to Buchman.

After his return to China from San Francisco Zhu Xuefan was not given travel permission again, so Bill was unable to keep in personal contact with him. In 1949 he became Minister of Communications in Mao Zedong's cabinet, and Bill did not write to him at all, as in the time of the Cultural Revolution to have done so would have put his friend at risk. But the friendship did not die – it was to lie dormant for about 40 years.

*   *   *   *   *

The endings of the war in Europe in 1945 and the war with Japan in 1946 were momentous. In the spring of 1946 Buchman met in Los Angeles with the team of 200 or so who had worked together in America during the war years. They were joined by all those who had been in the services and survived the war, and who were released early by order of General Marshall.

Over a period of days conferring together Buchman made the decision to move back to Europe, into countries that would have to find the will and the means to pick themselves up after six years of war.

Bill discovered that Buchman wanted him to be part of the group scheduled to return to Europe. The sailing date was six weeks off, and he himself felt he needed to take a very important step. He wanted to ask me to marry him. Everyone around us could see that we were very much in love, but Bill told me later that he did not propose to me any earlier because, 'I didn't know if you would accept me.'

One or two of his close friends helped him work out how to get me alone. 'Just ask her to drive you to visit one of the union officials,' someone suggested. So he approached me, and asked if I would drive him to Santa Monica that afternoon. I quickly agreed, of course, and went to get the car, thinking it would be packed full of Bill and his friends. To my surprise only Bill climbed in, and most unusually for him, he was sporting a flower in his buttonhole.

It was a 20-mile drive, and Bill asked me to turn off on a road by the Pacific Ocean. There, under the palm trees, he asked me to marry him. I never gave him a proper answer, but just fell into his arms.

We telephoned my parents in Philadelphia when we got back, and Bill found himself caught up in all the whirl of wedding plans. From that moment it was fast forward. It had to be, for in four weeks we had to travel the 3,000 miles by train across the country, send out the invitations, get a trousseau, plan the wedding party, get married, have a honeymoon (very short), and get on board the *Queen Mary* bound for Southampton.

We wanted to include as many people as possible, so it was a large church wedding of 500 guests, with 200 for the reception in a downtown hotel. There were eight bridesmaids and ten ushers. My father gave a luncheon for Bill and his groomsmen at The Union League Club, whose membership was open only to Republicans. No Democrats acceptable. The irony did not escape Bill, with his labour background.

After an all-too-brief honeymoon in the Pennsylvania mountains, Bill and I found ourselves in a curtained berth on the *Queen Mary*, which was still fitted out as a troopship, having only just been derequisitioned. In the seven years since Bill crossed the Atlantic to America he had left his mark in the lives of hundreds of men and women, friends who would keep in touch with him for the rest of his life, and whom he would never forget. Many felt a painful tug at their hearts as he sailed away.

And he was returning without Annie, but with a very new bride.

VII

Back to Britain

Bill Jaeger to his brother-in-law, Warner Clark:

London, May 24, 1946: 'Dear Warner, Life in America was busy. Life in Britain is busier. We have been married five weeks today. This morning we met 22 Swedish trade unionists and employers who are in London for training in British industry.

'It was wonderful to be on the *Queen Mary*, although she was still fitted out for the army. We had bunks suspended in mid-air and had to climb on a chair to get into them, no door to our cabin – just a curtain.

'It was moving to come up from Southampton to London, to see the damage done by the blitz and all the air-raid shelters in so many back yards and gardens.

'We have been in touch with 14 Members of Parliament, and 18 mayors in London. The three MPs for Birmingham gave our labour team a luncheon in the House of Commons, first of all taking us around the House, including seeing all the bomb damage. Click saw her first English Lord walking on the terrace by the Thames.

'We have been out to East London, which is a tragic sight. The ruins and the wreckage are everywhere, and it is amazing what the people there must have gone through.'

Bill was 34 years old when we got married. I was 36. What to do when you disagree? After the euphoria of getting married, it was a shock to us both the first time we differed.

It was about the number of thank-you letters for wedding presents. Bill, with his passion for numbers, calculated a number that I felt was far too low, and diminished what seemed to me to be an enormous task. Each of us felt in the other a 'will not budge' attitude.

Actually, Bill just loved to count. He delighted in adding up the numbers of appointments he had in a day, or the number of cities he had recently visited. He amazed me one day by telling me how many polka dots there were on a skirt I was wearing ... some sleight of eye to do with mentally dividing it into squares and then multiplying.

That first shipboard 'discussion' was quite a shock, but it was forgotten in the overwhelming reception our party was given by friends in England. Those Bill had worked with in East London thronged round him, so pleased to have him back again.

He heard first hand of the things they had been through in those long years, under bombardment night after night. The house where he had lived had gone, completely bombed out, and the papers and books also gone.

Once again a working group gathered around Bill. Already there was the nucleus who had come with us from America: Duncan, Blyth Ramsay, Tom Gillespie, Ros and June. Many of Bill's former colleagues from East London joined us. Two of them had worked down the mines during the war. Some came over from France and Holland as well. Several men recently demobilised from the armed forces also joined us.

Bill and I met with this group every day. We were staying in a large, comfortable room in one of the houses purchased by MRA at a very low rate at the end of the war. It seemed perfectly natural to Bill that 20 people should flock into our bedroom for a meeting, and that his new wife would provide tea for them all. Actually, I quite enjoyed it, having understood long since that life with Bill would often involve crowds of people.

* * * * *

Britain was faced with a massive rehabilitation programme. It was estimated that about a third of all British homes had been damaged or destroyed in the war, and industrial plants had been similarly depleted. Exports were urgently needed, but without industrial capacity the situation was close to being a vicious circle.

Ernest Bevin, Foreign Secretary in the Labour government, told the miners, 'Give me 30 million tons of coal for export and I will give you a foreign policy.'

Buchman heard from Will Locke, a miner and former Lord Mayor of Newcastle, that the coal industry was not in a healthy state. 'There is a discontent which is above man's power to alter,' Locke wrote, 'but we must try and reach the rank and file as best we can. The MRA spirit is needed.'

Meeting with his colleagues to plan steps that might be taken, Buchman's response to this letter was, 'Coal is the key.' And he believed he had the tailor-made method for doing as Locke asked.

A three-act play, *The Forgotten Factor*, had been written and performed to great effect in America in many industrial areas previously visited by *You Can Defend America*. The author was Alan Thornhill, a former Oxford don and long-time colleague of Buchman's.

The play described the internal conflicts of industry, which so often held up production, the bitter class war and hatred between management and labour, and the resulting mistrust. It also highlighted the divisive manipulations and threats used by some subversive groups in order to get control. It offered hope of a genuine solution and a way forward for labour and management together, through openness and honesty, and the search for what is right not who is right.

83

It was ideal for the situation in British industry. Initially it was put on in London, and miners from several coalfields came to see it there. Among them were four from Doncaster, in the Yorkshire coal heartland, who then arranged for the play to be staged in their area six weeks later. One Doncaster miner wrote afterwards, 'If the spirit of the play is put into practice, teamwork in the Doncaster mines will become the pattern for the country.'

Bill and I spent a week in Doncaster, meeting people from the mining community and inviting them to come and see the play. The theatre was packed out night after night.

Stockport, Bill's home town, is not many miles west of Doncaster, and Bill took me there to meet his relatives and to show me the place I had heard Annie and him talk about for so many years.

We spent three days there, and for me the most moving time was a visit to the house where Annie had lived and Bill had grown up. It was such a world away from my own background.

Our train drew in to Stockport station just after sunset, and as we stepped out the air was soft and wet, laden with the smell of coal dust. A small laughing woman with white hair and blue eyes rushed towards us. It could have been Annie. It was her sister, Auntie Alice. She and her husband fairly jumped at us, embracing us, talking and laughing with such vivacity. I loved them immediately.

The next day we walked about a mile, past rows and rows of silent houses, to the area where Bill was born and grew up.

There was little traffic on the streets, petrol being rationed. No one in Bill's family had ever owned a car. Finally we came to the shop. Dingy and dusty, the whole building was about twelve feet wide. The new owner let us inside. We saw the back room, which Bill explained to me was their one living room, where they ate, sat and Annie cooked. It was about eight feet square. Beyond was the scullery, with its sloping roof. It had a sink and one cold water tap. We went upstairs – narrow, steep wooden stairs. At the top the front room looked out on the cobbled street. A tiny little box of a room adjoined it – Bill's room.

Returning to Doncaster, Bill and I were put up in a miner's home. It was raining and really cold, even though it was June. We all started to converge on a village hall for tea. As I stood in the rain, waiting for Bill to finish his conversation with one of the miners, I heard a voice at my shoulder, 'It's a long way from Philadelphia, isn't it?'

I turned, and saw Frank Buchman smiling at me. I must have been looking pretty glum – it was nice to know that someone understood the way I felt.

*　　*　　*　　*　　*

Back in London several weeks later, Bill told me that our next journey would be to Switzerland.

Neutral Switzerland had been spared the wartime suffering and cruelties inflicted on so much of Europe. There was a large MRA team in Switzerland, who had kept in touch with Buchman throughout the war. In 1946 a group of them expressed the hope that Switzerland might be a place where Europeans could gather to rebuild Europe, from the rubble of the bombs and from the more painful results of occupation.

What was needed, the Swiss MRA team decided, was a conference centre where Europeans could plan together for the future with people from all parts of the world.

Such a place was eventually found. The former 'Caux Palace Hotel', above Montreux and overlooking Lake Geneva, once a luxury hotel, by the end of the war was in a derelict condition. It had been used by refugees from all over Europe. The asking price was very low. One hundred and fifty Swiss, many of them at great personal sacrifice, raised the sum required to purchase the building. Several gave their entire fortunes. Families from all over the country committed themselves not only to restoring the building, but to providing the manpower to outfit and run it.

The opening MRA international conference there was in July, 1946. Quite a large party was travelling from London, by way of the boat train to Dover, the Channel crossing, and the overnight train via Paris to Switzerland. Bill and I were among the group.

We were wakened early as the train came to a shuddering halt at the border between France and Switzerland, and instructed to alight, taking our passports for examination. There was a station café on the platform, and any initial annoyance at being wakened by officialdom turned to bliss when Swiss breakfast arrived. The sun shone bright and warm, and the crisp rolls and croissants melted in the mouth; there were beautiful swirls of real butter, black cherry jam and absolutely delicious real coffee. The contrast between this and the kind of food available in postwar England was all too vivid. But how everyone enjoyed it.

Buses awaited the train's arrival at Montreux, and then began a tortuous, winding ascent up the mountainside on a long series of hairpin curves. About halfway up the party caught the exciting first glimpse of the old hotel, now renamed 'Mountain House'. Somehow a fairytale image came to mind, as we saw the large building with its silhouetted spires and turrets.

It took almost an hour to make the ascent, and as the buses drove up to the entrance the travellers were greeted by singing from a large choir. Dressed in their colourful national costumes, the chorus seemed to represent the whole world.

By the time of the arrival of the group from London, the building had been transformed by an army of volunteer workers from all over Europe. Many were pre-war friends of Bill's. Having scoured, painted, decorated and cleaned up the huge building, these same people were now doing the everyday tasks of bedmaking, cooking, and serving up the meals in the big dining room.

During those first hours Bill caught up with old friends, and heard a little of what some of them had gone through when their countries had been occupied.

Buchman had arrived a few days before the large group from London, and had been given the same reception at the front entrance from the Swiss hosts, the international chorus and scores of old friends whom he had not seen for seven years.

He stood in the doorway, deeply moved, looking from face to face at friends from France, Denmark, Norway, Holland, whose countries had lived under German occupation, some who had been in concentration camps, and many who had known starvation and in some cases torture.

The conference was officially opened on the following day, at which time Buchman spoke to them and thanked them for their farsighted planning in acquiring Mountain House. Then he said, 'But where are the Germans? You will never rebuild Europe without Germany.'

There was a stunned silence.

To the eternal credit of some of those present, soon wheels were set in motion with the Allied authorities, and within a few weeks 16 Germans were given permission to leave Germany and go to Caux. Many of them were old friends of Buchman's, who had fought courageously to keep their faith and beliefs alive in Nazi Germany.

The rooms at Caux were full for two months that summer. Many of the visitors were coalminers from Britain, contacted through performances of *The Forgotten Factor*, and who had set up a special travel fund for the purpose.

* * * * *

In October *The Forgotten Factor* opened at MRA's newly acquired Westminster Theatre in London, and busloads of miners, managers and later Coal Board officials came night after night to see it. Output in countless mines was significantly improved as a result of the new spirit abroad in the coalfields, and the play was then taken on tour round Britain.

Bill and I returned to England after the Caux summer conference. I was four months pregnant. England was grim in that coldest winter for 60 years. Electricity cuts combined with the bitter cold to make it hard to keep warm. Everything was still rationed, and obtained through coupons – clothes, food and petrol.

Bill and I managed to go to the movies about once a week. In those post-war years the large and ornate picture palaces packed them in, as people sought a little respite from the grim austerity the war had brought. Afterwards we would go for a meal, though the menus were rather limited. We would often choose omelettes, made with powdered egg.

A week before the baby was due, Bill came home with a hyacinth plant which looked as if it might come into bloom any day. When I woke up a few days later its scent filled the room, and reminded me of Easter at home, when Dad always used to give me a hyacinth.

The next day, in mid-February, 1947, our son was born. I woke Bill in the night, and he sprang out of bed and rushed to the cupboard and began pulling on his clothes with terrific speed, ending up in his best suit, with his hair brushed, ready to get going. Actually, it was many more hours before we even went off to the hospital, but his anxiety about being late touched me very much.

We called our son Frederic William, after my father, and after Bill. It actually rather pleased Bill that there had been a German Emperor of the same name.

Some friends gave us an impressively large English pram, and Bill, the proud new father in a blue pinstripe suit, was to be seen many an afternoon, pushing it through Green Park, with his American hat pulled down firmly on his head.

VIII

Post-war Germany

Throughout the months since the Caux summer conference of 1946 a real advance had been made towards answering Buchman's question, 'Where are the Germans?'

Due largely to the initiative of one of Buchman's oldest American colleagues, Kenaston Twitchell, Allied permission for an MRA party to enter occupied Germany was step by step obtained. Twitchell's father-in-law was a US Senator, and through him an interview was obtained with the US Secretary of State, General Marshall. Visas for Twitchell and his wife to enter the American zone in Germany were granted.

In London, en route to Germany, Twitchell had an interview with Lord Pakenham, who was in charge of the British zone in Germany. He said to Twitchell, 'Along with food, the kind of work you are doing is the only thing that will do any good in Germany now.'

What the military and political leaders were aware of was the importance of the morale of the nation. Germany's cities were in ruins, especially Berlin and the industrial area of the Ruhr. Nazism was dead, but Communism had quickly filled the vacuum. Stalin had split the country into two by persuading the Allies that it should be his Russian army that would march into Berlin.

To help with German translation, the Twitchells were

accompanied by Eugene von Teuber, a Sudetenland Austrian whose family had had to flee their homeland. Many months were spent visiting the major cities of Germany, always with the support of those in charge of the American and British zones.

Towards the end of the time General Lucius Clay, who commanded the American zone, arranged a press conference for Twitchell and his group with German journalists, and after that with the German political leaders of the four Länder (states) of the American zone.

Twitchell told them about Caux and issued, in the name of Buchman, an invitation to come as guests to the summer conference now in session there, and to bring their families with them. He also suggested they might draw up a list of other men and women in their Lands who would profit from such a visit.

*   *   *   *   *

That summer, 1947, the Caux conference had started in June, and the Jaeger family had driven to Switzerland from London with friends who also had a new baby.

Bill had lately come across a young man he felt was a natural for the labour and industrial work. He was Gordon Wise, son of the Labour Premier of Western Australia. Gordon had been a pilot in the Royal Australian Air Force during the war, had met MRA and become convinced of its importance, and was also attending the Caux summer conference.

Bill invited Gordon to go with him on visits from Caux to meet some of the Swiss trade union leadership, and then at the end of the summer asked him if he would be willing to work with him in Britain that winter.

Gordon accepted, and turned out to be a most valued colleague. He was a charming, gregarious young man, with thick, curly blonde hair, blue eyes and an innate grasp of the political and ideological issues. Gordon was to work closely with Bill for the next five years, supporting him in many different ways, by his understanding of issues they were grappling with, and by his willingness to be on hand night and day to take Bill anywhere, even quite often at midnight to pick up the early editions of the papers.

Towards the end of August it was announced to the conference that a specially invited party of Germans, about 150 in all, would shortly be arriving.

When the day came, Bill and I were among the 700 at the assembly who packed into the great hall to await the arrival.

Buchman was an artist. He had an eye for effect. He understood the importance of creating an appropriate atmosphere for different occasions. We were assembled in the old hotel's largest reception room, decorated in almost baroque style, with a high vaulted ceiling and a great brass chandelier. The large choir, in their national costumes, were in place on the low stage at the front of the hall.

Word came that the buses had arrived. A strange hush came over the room, and then in a few minutes the German group were ushered through the doors by their Swiss hosts. The Germans moved slowly forward, eyes cast down, their clothes quite noticeably shabby.

The packed room watched silently as the party were settled into the seats of honour reserved for them. When all were seated the choir stood up, and suddenly a song written for the occasion, in German, with music by a young Norwegian, burst forth. Uncertain at first, the audience rose as well.

From that day on many began to glimpse how a new Germany might come into being. It was an objective that went deep into Bill's thinking and planning. He met many of the Germans who came to Caux and felt at home with them. The language seemed to come naturally to him. Strange, after those experiences he had had as a small boy.

* * * * *

Now that the initial steps had been taken, Buchman arranged for a strong international party to move into Germany. Two of those who undertook major responsibility for the enterprise were Erich and Emmy Peyer, a German-speaking Swiss couple. They were joined by some of Buchman's most senior colleagues.

Throughout the year of 1947-48 this pioneering group were able to meet a number of remarkable Germans who saw in Buchman's concept of Moral Re-Armament a programme that could help to rebuild their devastated country.

Some of them had already seen the MRA musical, *The Good Road*, dramatising the spiritual heritage of the West. The show had a large cast of 200 from many countries. A German translation of *The Forgotten Factor* was also prepared for use.

The summer of 1948 saw a steady stream of Germans coming to Caux, among them the former mayor of Cologne, Konrad Adenauer, now president of the Parliamentary Council of the three Western Zones.

'I have been completely convinced of the great value of Caux,' he said.

In September, 1948, Frank Buchman received the following telegram from Dr Karl Arnold, the Minister President of North Rhine/Westphalia:

'The members of the Government of North Rhine/Westphalia, who by your kind invitation were able to take part in your work at Caux, have expressed the wish that the Government invite you to extend your work to North Rhine/Westphalia and particularly in the Ruhr area. The Government has unanimously agreed to this proposal. We would be most happy if you, Dr Buchman, with your international team, could through performances of *The Good Road* and *The Forgotten Factor* spread the message and spirit of Caux in our land, and thereby help give our nation new hope and strength.'

Bill and I were delighted when it was agreed that we were to be among the party of 200 who were to make this historic trip into Germany. Duncan Corcoran was going too, as was Gordon Wise.

Food and housing would be in short supply, so essential needs were taken care of by General Clay. The MRA group which went into Germany were given US Army status of 'Information Division', which meant the cast and those of us with the supporting company could buy at the PX and have meals at the officers' mess. Army buses and staff cars provided transport. Posters were put up in the midst of the rubble, advertising the play, and it was performed over a period of almost three weeks in Munich, Stuttgart, Frankfurt, Düsseldorf and Essen.

*   *   *   *   *

By the end of 1948 what had been described as 'the spirit of Caux' was beginning to take root and grow in the lives of many individual Germans. The need now was to nurture this new life to fruition.

Among the first to undertake this were two young Norwegians, Jens Wilhelmsen and Leif Hovelsen, who had been in the Norwegian Resistance during the War. Hovelsen had been captured and tortured by the Gestapo. 'The spirit of Caux' and Moral Re-Armament meant for him a willingness to uproot the hatred towards Germany that he carried in his heart. In very concrete terms this took effect when he went to the Ruhr to help with the work of rebuilding the morale of the German nation.

Because of openings created in the industrial heartland of the Ruhr by performances of *The Good Road*, those who undertook this delicate work with the ordinary people of Germany soon were swept into the lives of those in the industrial, political and cultural life of the country. They were guests of unions, went down coalmines, spoke with management and politicians about the rebuilding programme that was needed. The Germans took them into their homes, where they sometimes slept in rooms with holes in the window stuffed with newspaper or rags. Their

German hosts shared their small food rations with them. Gradually the men and women of Buchman's international group – Hovelsen among them – came to understand some of the deepest feelings of their hosts. So many lived with total misery, cynicism and bitter disillusionment.

*   *   *   *   *

Late in December, 1948, Bill came into our London room and showed me the telegram he was holding. It was from Buchman, asking if he would join up with the party in the Ruhr, and, as Buchman put it, 'dig in to the work there' as soon as possible.

Bill was totally unprepared for the storm that was unleashed. 'Oh no! No! No! No!' I cried.

This would be the first time we would be separated, and I was quite unprepared for such a thing. On my mind was our baby son, and the support Bill had always given to us both. Quite simply, also, I was quite homesick in England, and without Bill around I felt lost.

My vehemence paralysed him. Into his mind there flashed the memory of the time when he had heard his mother strike out at his father, in her desperation to be understood. Not knowing how to react to me, Bill stood and listened, trying to control the panic feelings sweeping over him. He loved his wife dearly, but he knew also that he would go to Germany.

Finally I agreed to his going, on condition that I took Frederic back to America and stayed with my parents until we could all be together again. This was what we arranged to do.

*   *   *   *   *

When Bill set off for Germany, Duncan Corcoran and Gordon Wise accompanied him in a small car, together with Martin Flütsch, a Swiss who had offered to act as translator. It was to be a six-month, non-stop campaign.

94

The Chairman of the German Coal Board, Dr Heinrich Kost, who was Managing Director of the Rheinpreusen mining company in Moers, had invited Buchman to bring the German version of *The Forgotten Factor* to his area, for which Bill's carload were part of the preparation group.

As they entered the Ruhr, they were greeted by a shocking sight: 80% of Essen, for instance, was destroyed. There was ruin and rubble everywhere. Few street signs existed, and it was extremely difficult to find one's way around, especially at night with no street lights. It would have been impossible for Bill and his group, except for the careful forward planning that had taken place.

Bill and his friends had worked out three means of approach. The first, and most obvious, was inviting people to see *The Forgotten Factor*. The second was meeting for debate in taverns and working men's halls with people who had seen the play or who wanted to know more about how to rebuild the life of their country and their people. The third was simply living in the homes of the miners and others in the different cities. Conversations with the families could go on long into the night. It was the same individual work that had taken place in the East End of London, and in Detroit and all across America.

Bill, Duncan and Gordon linked up with people who had been working in Germany during the previous year, among them the young Norwegians, Leif Hovelsen and Jens Wilhelmsen, Bernard Hallward, a Canadian businessman, and Takasumi Mitsui, from one of the leading industrial families of Japan.

Together they comprised a unique and powerful panel of speakers.

Another important contribution, almost a secret weapon, was that of Mme Irène Laure, former leader of the Socialist Women of France, and a wartime resistance leader. She had a consuming hatred of all Germans until a visit to Caux where she met the widow of Adam von Trott, one of the leaders of the failed bomb plot against

Hitler. Von Trott had been caught and hanged. The two women talked on more than one occasion. Mme Laure met other Germans as well, and began to realise that a hate-consumed person could not possibly hope to bring reconstruction to Europe, for Europe must include Germany.

Mme Laure travelled to the Ruhr with her husband, Victor, who was one of the founders of the Marxist Seamen's Union of France. When she saw the destruction of the cities of the Ruhr, and later Berlin, and the hundreds of women at work all day trying to clear the piles of rubble with their bare hands, Irène Laure's heart completely melted.

At meetings, speaking in French with German translation, the heart of her message was to ask the forgiveness of her listeners, forgiveness for the hatred she had carried in her heart. She said she had wanted to see Germany erased from the map of Europe. Few German audiences could ignore such a heartfelt plea.

* * * * *

When *The Forgotten Factor* opened in Moers in January, 1949, Bill and the rest of the speakers went along to a tavern on the outskirts of the town. They had been invited there to meet with Max Bladeck and Paul Kurowski, two of the town's leading Communist functionaries. These men turned up with some of the keenest debaters in the Party, with the declared aim of 'sinking the MRA panel with all hands'. Six of them spoke one after the other.

The MRA panel then had the chance to reply, starting with Duncan and Bill. The meeting went on for four hours.

The debate that evening was the beginning for Bladeck and Kurowski of a new line of thought – 'human nature can be changed'. It stuck in their minds, and suggested there was an alternative to the class struggle, an alternative that was neither capitalist nor Communist.

As a result of the Ruhr campaign, Max Bladeck, the

Clara Clark.
wept into the life
Bill's group.'

15 Backstage with the patriotic revue *You Can Defend America*, Bill briefs the cast on who is in the audience.

16 Detroit, June 17, 1942. Workers at Briggs Bodies, engaged in tank production, listen to MRA speakers during the lunch break. Bill and Duncan Corcoran watch from beneath the corner of the podium.

17 Annie Jaeger visited by her son Bill, during her final illness

18 Zhu Xuefan (centre), China's delegate to the 1944 conference of the ILO in Philadelphia, met Bill Jaeger there for the first time. Bill took him into American homes.

19 Philadelphia, June, 1945. Bill Jaeger and Clara Clark celebrate their engagement. *Front row*: Stuart Smith, Paul Hogue, Adam McLean, Clara, Bill, Eli Bager, Duncan Corcoran, 'Scotty' Macfarlane. *Back row*: Lee Vrooman, Polly Ann Eastman, Denise Hyde, Tom Gillespie, Ros Lombard, Warner Clark, June Lee, Jim Cooper, Blyth Ramsay, Edith Shillington, Dot Ensor

Moers Communist leader, became committed to the ideas and spirit of MRA. He, like many another, had his struggles and his lapses, but he was most assuredly an example of how a Communist can change. His co-worker, Paul Kurowski, described what it meant.

'I was undergirded safely for many years by the Communist ideology; this faith carried me in difficult and dangerous circumstances. But despite that faith I began to have doubts ... I saw that people showed frailties and weaknesses. The difference between theory and practice, but above all self-advancement, still played too big a role....

'This however completely changed when, through meeting men and women of Moral Re-Armament, I came to know this ideology's completely different aims ... my thinking changed when I experienced in silence the totality of God's absolute standards, and also the power of an ideologically lived-out faith ... When a person passionately takes on a total commitment under God's guidance, his thinking and his entire nature change. We miss the meaning of life if we want to stay as we are.'

Many Communists underwent a similar change, finding in Moral Re-Armament a more profound philosophy. The West German Communist party removed 40 of its regional leaders, including the chairman of the Ruhr regional committee, Hugo Paul, for having dealings with a contrary ideology.

The Executive of the Communist Party of West Germany was summoned on January 8, 1950, to a special conference in Düsseldorf at which they were told that the entire Executive and Secretariat was to be reorganised because it had been 'tainted with an ideology inimical to the Party'.

The Manchester Guardian on February 8, 1950, reported on these changes under the heading 'A New Communist Heresy – Moral Re-Armament'.

*　　*　　*　　*　　*

Gordon Wise said Bill hammered out a philosophy in those months which attracted Marxists, but went far beyond Marxism. Some of that philosophy was incorporated in a world broadcast made by Frank Buchman in June of that year: such basic thoughts as 'MRA believes in the full dimension of change, economic change, social change, national change and international change, all based on personal change.'

The group addressed every executive of the Socialist Party in the Ruhr area. They met the union men in the bombed-out factories. They travelled daily up and down the famous autobahn linking the great Ruhr cities.

Gordon Wise said that Bill provided generalship for that phase of MRA's work in the Ruhr. Sometimes when *The Forgotten Factor* was being shown in a particular town, the group would meet together with no onward programme at all, which meant no food and nowhere to sleep, quite apart from nothing to do. Bill would ask about the neighbouring towns, and who knew someone in them. If someone said they knew the mayor or some other dignitary, this person would be despatched to go and offer to bring the play. Thus the programme unfolded and rolled along.

Bill, Duncan and Gordon, Mme Laure, and the management men on the panel of speakers, addressed 11 of the 12 Land Parliaments, visiting most of the major towns of West Germany. They stayed in homes or small inns, and were lucky to get a boiled egg for breakfast occasionally. When the play was hosted by a mining company, and where rationing was still tight, the evening meal would consist of a bowl of thick soup and bread. The cast and company would have a supplement from American food parcels, opened backstage and eaten during the interval.

Germany's astonishing post-war recovery became known worldwide as 'The German Miracle'. Buchman's decision to offer the hope of a new way forward to the country made its contribution to that recovery.

Dr Hans Boeckler, President of the newly formed Trade

Union Congress (DGB), attended a conference at Caux in 1949, where he said, 'When man changes, the structure of society changes. When the structure of society changes, men change. Both go together, and both are necessary.'

IX

1950s America

The months in Germany bore fruit in other ways as well. Gordon Wise commented later, 'I learned many lessons from Bill in Germany. One evening we arrived late at a trade union office, and it was obviously closed. Bill, however, told me to go over and knock at the door. I did so reluctantly, and came back and said it was closed. Bill said he thought I should persist, because he felt somebody would be there. Even more reluctantly I tried again. Eventually the door opened, and thanks to Martin Flütsch I discovered that this was the janitor. Bill joined us, and we had quite a conversation with the man.

'Afterwards Bill said, "See what we would have missed if you hadn't gone back and we hadn't met that janitor." He would not take no for an answer if he was convinced about something.

'I learned to respect Bill's questions or wonderings which the Spirit seemed to impart to him, without dismissing his enquiries as being either uncomplimentary or untrusting on his part. This experience has helped me for the rest of my life.'

At the end of every day, before turning in, Bill wrote me either a letter or a postcard. He made notes about his interviews as he went along during the day, and before sleeping he would copy these notes from the backs of envelopes and such like to other paper, to use in future times.

By the end of June, 1949, Bill sent word to me in America that he would be at Caux for the summer conference, and so Frederic and I should return to Europe and join him in Switzerland. The reunion that took place was marred somewhat because I had hoped Bill himself would be waiting for us when the ship docked in Cherbourg. Instead I found he had asked a young man to meet and look after his wife and baby, and put us on the train for Switzerland.

When we eventually met, Bill was surprised at my outburst, and could find nothing to say in his own defence. But the feelings, once aired, soon blew away.

* * * * *

Bill took his family back to England at the end of the summer, and we based in London for the next two years.

Just as the coalmines were one major focus for Bill's work in Britain after the war, another was the docks.

The old East London Bill had known had been bombed out of existence by nightly Luftwaffe raids. There was much rebuilding needed, in reclaiming the ruins, and in supporting a population which had borne the brunt of the bombing.

A British couple who joined Bill were Don and Connie Simpson. They took a house in Bermondsey, in the London dockland, to act as base and headquarters. Two Irishmen, Eric Turpin and Alec Porter, also came, and through their commitment the East London labour work was regenerated after the war, this time centring especially on the dockworkers. Most evenings saw a group of people, Bill among them, going down from the West End of London to join those visiting homes in dockland.

* * * * *

In the summer of 1953, while again at Caux, Bill received a cable from American colleagues, asking if he could come to the States and stand by John Riffe, who was up for election to the important post of Executive Vice-President of the CIO (Congress of Industrial Organisations).

Bill felt the next weeks and months could prove to be vitally important in the world of American labour, and that he would be glad to go and help in any way he could. Within two days he was on a plane, flying the Atlantic. He arranged for me and Frederic, now six, to follow later by boat.

It had been 12 years since he had first met Riffe, in California. He had kept in touch with him, and knew from Charles Haines and others of John's many ups and downs, both in his organising work and in his family affairs. Only recently Bill had heard the good news that John had finally been able to break completely with the self-destructive habits of a lifetime.

Not long after John had made his decision to live differently, Allan Hayward, Executive Vice-President of the CIO, died and Riffe's name was put forward by many of his colleagues to fill the position. The Executive Board eventually gave a unanimous acceptance of his nomination.

Riffe's nomination was due to be accepted by the full congress at the annual CIO convention in a few weeks' time, but even though he had been unanimously elected by the Executive Board, his candidacy had received some counter-attacks.

Riffe had run into a Communist-inspired onslaught which had its roots outside America.

In the years 1946-1953 MRA had greatly extended its contacts with union leaders and their work across the world. Stalin and his followers at that time were forcefully propagating the Marxist concept. The Cold War was at its height. Through the trades unions, management and government, MRA offered a realistic alternative to the class struggle – a struggle taking place in the coalmines, the steel industry, aircraft manufacturing, the docks, car industries and engineering in Europe and in America, as well as in the Latin American countries and Africa and Asia.

103

The World Federation of Trade Unions, founded in 1945, was meant to unite the world of labour after the Second World War, but very soon the Marxists wanted to take control of it. The result was that in 1949 the ICFTU (International Congress of Free Trade Unions) was founded. The British and American Federations of Labour, and those in Scandinavia and Holland, split from the WFTU and formed the ICFTU.

Paul Finet of Belgium, was the first President of the ICFTU and came to the MRA summer conference at Caux in 1949; so did Evert Kupers of the Executive Board of the Dutch Federation of Labour, Konrad Ilg, General Secretary of the International Metal Workers, who visited Caux in 1946, and August Cool, the General Secretary of the Catholic Federation of Labour.

A severe attack from the Marxists in industrial circles across the world followed these high level visits to MRA's world assembly, because the new understanding the men received while at Caux posed a threat to the Marxists' plans for domination of world labour.

In 1952 a large MRA group was invited to India by a committee which included the General Secretary of the Indian National TUC. One of those who was quick to respond was Sibnath Banerjee, who was then President of the Hind Mazdoor Sabha, and had been a sincere and committed Marxist.

Unknown to him his General Secretary, Dinkar Desai, wrote innocently to the ICFTU HQ in Brussels, asking for information about MRA because of the interest shown in it among the Indian workers and the unions, following the visit of the MRA group.

The ICFTU itself was very much anti-Communist, but there were individuals in it who were Marxist. Some of these Marxists seized on Dinkar Desai's enquiry as an opportunity to express their hostility. They sent an enquiry out to their membership across the world, following which the press office of the ICFTU issued a statement. Though the matter never came up in a full session of the ICFTU annual conference in 1953, it was, however, purported to have been so presented. The statement recommended 'that Free Trade Unions would do well to be on their guard against MRA'. This report was sent out to all ICFTU affiliates worldwide.

Hearing of this while visiting Caux in 1953, Banerjee was astonished that his organisation was quoted as having requested the report, as he had no knowledge of it. In the light of his firm and positive conviction about MRA, he went to meet various European trade union leaders – he attended the British Trade Union Congress meeting in Brighton – and made his views known. He visited his opposite numbers in Scandinavia, Belgium, France, and Italy to clarify the situation.

Later from his home base in Calcutta he issued a statement of refutation of the ICFTU report, with his convictions, which he sent to all affiliates.

However, Bill and his friends realised that the report had made a head start and their work of building sound labour-management relations was being seriously handicapped. At the same time, they acknowledged that some of those in MRA had tended to overstate their achievements, sometimes misquoting comments made by national trade union leaders about MRA.

In the spring of 1953, nine broadcasts against Moral Re-Armament had been made by Moscow and Tashkent Radios.

'Moral Re-Armament has been working on an ideological front for several decades,' said one of the broadcasts. 'It has the power to win over radical, revolutionary minds. It is replacing the concept of the class struggle by that of the eternal struggle between good and evil... It has established bridgeheads in every continent... It has now started on its decisive phase of total expansion throughout the world.'

It was only two days after the publication of the ICFTU

report in 1953 that John Riffe was singled out for bitter attack in certain New York newspapers, on the grounds of his association with MRA.

* * * * *

Shortly after arriving in the USA, Bill was driven by George Vondermuhll to Arlington, Virginia, to the white clapboard house where the Riffe family lived.

Bill found his old friend a mellow, humble man, massive in build but gentle in his manner. He was only 49, and in the previous years had won many victories for the Steelworkers, but there had been a price to be paid, especially in his health.

John brought Bill and George up to date on the situation which would shortly face him at the CIO annual convention. 'It doesn't really bother me,' said John, 'we'll just see how the chips fall.' He had already made up his mind how to play it. He had a high-powered weapon in his armoury – honesty.

Riffe sat through the convention, waiting for the question of the candidacy for Executive Vice-President. When the time came, many speakers attacked him because of his association with MRA, but equally as many gave him their support.

The Chairman offered John the chance to explain his position. Riffe began quietly,

'Some of you have met people in Moral Re-Armament. Some of you haven't. Well, you're looking at one now. You all know me. You all know the kind of life I lived among you.'

The room was silent.

'When things seemed hopeless and I was at my worst,' Riffe continued, 'I found an answer to my problems through meeting Moral Re-Armament many years ago. But I held something back. You've seen me sitting around all night in poker games and then turning up next morning

106

bleary eyed when I should have been backing up my union colleagues.

'A year ago I really decided to face moral standards of absolute honesty, purity, unselfishness and love, and to accept the guidance of God every day. Since then everything has become different. I've not only had peace of mind and a happy home, but I've found a new sense of responsibility and dedication to my job and the labour movement. No resolution could change me. God changed me.

'Nobody can object to John Riffe quitting whisky and poker and a lot of other things he shouldn't have been doing. Now, if contact with MRA makes a union man like me honest and decent and with an unselfish love for his fellow men, is that interfering with labour? If it gives me a happy home life again, and makes me do my job with greater responsibility, is that hurting labour?

'Millions of our members in this country believe in these principles. There isn't a man in this room that wouldn't say they are right. But do we all live them? I certainly did not. We pass resolutions against Communism, but here is a force that is answering Communism by changing Communists.

'I'm in your hands. You must decide what you want to do. You have the power, you are perfectly free. No matter what you decide, my decision is made. No matter what you decide, I won't harbour any bitterness. I want always to be your friend.'

No one spoke. Finally one of the Executive Board rose and said, 'We've heard the Executive Vice-President. We know the way he has lived. We know his quality of life. I only wish I could live that way myself. I suggest we now go on to the next point on the agenda.'

The decision had been made.

*   *   *   *   *

George and Rosamund Vondermuhll suggested to Bill that

when his wife and son arrived in America they should all three move in with them, and share their Washington home. They had one son also, two years younger than Fred, and there would be plenty of room for all.

The house was near the Washington Cathedral, to which was attached an excellent private school for boys. With immense generosity the Vondermuhlls made it possible for Fred to attend that school, along with their own son. Fred happily and quickly became American at that school, and he and Alfred Vondermuhll grew up like brothers.

He soon developed a passion for baseball, and Bill heard from the school coach that Fred was being watched as a 'sleeper', having become a good pitcher in the junior team.

The Vondermuhll house provided us with a wonderful home, and this happy family unity continued up until 1959, coinciding with the beginnings of Fred's teenage years, and a change of living arrangements.

Those years were extremely full and busy ones, and involved many different elements of life in America at the time. One of the major issues was in regard to the changes taking place in race.

It was only 86 years since the end of the war between the states, which was supposed to have ended slavery. There were no slaves as such, but there was apartheid. Blacks were not allowed in restaurants or hotels. On buses, in street cars and in theatres they were assigned to their own section, separate from the whites. The jobs mostly available to them were menial, due to lack of education.

An important beginning had been made in this regard by a black teacher, the daughter of former slaves. Mrs Mary McLeod Bethune started with nothing but courage, will and faith, and founded a college for her people.

When Bill heard from some friends that Mrs Bethune was now living in Washington, we went to call upon her.

We found ourselves in the presence of a majestically gnarled, white-haired lady.

Bill told her about his background, about Annie, his mother, and also about his work with world labour, and why we were in Washington. Mrs Bethune gave us her perspectives on the changes that were taking place for her people, and those that were still needed in America. As we began to take our leave, Bill commented on the handsome walking stick she used.

'President Roosevelt gave me this,' she replied.

That summer Mrs Bethune was invited to attend an MRA conference being held at Mackinac Island, Michigan. She met Frank Buchman there.

At a conference in Washington in 1955 she said of MRA, 'To be a part of this great, uniting force is the crowning experience of my life.'

Some time later a musical play based on her life was written by Alan Thornhill, author of *The Forgotten Factor*. The show was entitled *The Crowning Experience*, and made history when it opened in Atlanta, Georgia. For the first time ever, blacks and whites entered the theatre by the same door and sat in unsegregated seats. The show moved to Washington and played for seven weeks to full houses at the National Theatre.

After meeting Mrs Bethune, and focusing on the fact that the country was beginning to undergo a profound change in racial attitudes, Bill did what he always did: set out to get to know the people involved. Taking one or two friends with him, he met many of the staff and students at the all-black Howard University. He introduced himself to members of the NAACP (National Association for the Advancement of Colored Peoples). In the labour field he made some close friends among the black leadership, one of whom was A Philips Randolph, President of the Sleeping Car Porters' Union.

*   *   *   *   *

109

The network of colleagues whom Bill had trained and worked with in different countries continued to spread to many parts of the world. Continually in touch by letter, they regularly exchanged information about the areas in which they were working. For example, an Englishman, Laurie Vogel, went to Brazil, where one of his aims was to get to know the South American unions. Those he met first were the dockers in the port of Sao Paolo. Soon he was joined by Luis Puig of Guatemala, whom Bill had met first at the ILO.

The Rio dockers lived with their families in wretched dwellings – shanty towns. For the different groups who made up the unions it was gunlaw. After a number of years working with these men, Vogel and Puig saw a remarkable change taking place. Guns were handed in, shanties were made habitable, and many couples went through the marriage ceremony, with all their children in attendance.

Some of the Brazilian dockers began to attend MRA conferences, and eventually a film, *Men of Brazil*, was made of their story about the transformation that had taken place.

The two Irishmen, Eric Turpin and Alec Porter, who had moved into East London dockland to help Bill's colleagues there, visited America in 1959, and went to meet some of the American dockworkers, in the International Longshoremen's Union. Turpin began in Brooklyn, New York, with the aim of offering to show the *Men of Brazil* film to the local union group.

He went to see the President of the Local, a man of some reputation, who passed him on to his vice-president, an enormous black man with a gravelly voice, who rejoiced in the name of Small.

Fred Small knew all about the ruthless, sometimes blackmailing, sometimes violent efforts used to control the votes and support of the Longshoremen. In order to survive, he had in the past gone along with them. But he was absolutely bowled over by the Brazilian film Turpin showed him, and by the stories he heard from the men and women of MRA. They opened a door to a better way for him, and for his union.

Fred Small became a stalwart supporter of Bill's work, travelling to many parts of the world, including South America, to give his convictions. He said about Bill, 'One of the best informed foreigners I've met. He understands the inner workings of people and therefore of organisations. He is a senior statesman as far as labour is concerned. He is an uplifting character. You can tell him anything and his advice is always good. I'm just glad he is my friend.'

*   *   *   *   *

Around the time of meeting Fred Small in 1957, Bill also developed a warm friendship with Harry van Arsdale, President of the New York City Central Labour Council, and President of Local 3 Electrical Union in New York. They kept in touch, and some years later van Arsdale attended a Caux conference with some of his union leadership.

*   *   *   *   *

Meanwhile, John Riffe continued to fill the role of statesman, not only in his position of Executive Vice-President of the CIO until its amalgamation with the AFL, but in his outreach into fields other than labour.

In 1954 President Eisenhower asked Riffe to call on him, and they talked for over an hour. Riffe said later: 'The President was interested in my thinking as a labour man. He wanted to know what had happened to an ordinary guy, a labour guy like me, to make me take such a new attitude to my job, and to the bosses.

'We laughed when he suggested it was unusual for him

111

to be able to sit and talk in this man-to-man way with a hardened Democrat.

'He was most interested in my stories of Communists being changed. We talked about Asia and Africa also. He could see that what happened in those continents would affect the whole world, and he asked me to keep him posted with any further news I might get. It was a great time.'

John Riffe died from a long-term heart condition early in 1958, but not before he had realised an ambition to visit Caux.

*　　*　　*　　*　　*

Ten years after the misinformation and misunderstandings about MRA were issued in the ICFTU report from Stockholm, Bill and Gordon Wise were able to get the records put straight.

In Britain one of Bill's long-term friends was the General Secretary of the Agricultural Workers' Union, Harold Collison, later Lord Collison. He was so convinced of the value of MRA, and so indignant that a serious injustice had been done by the ICFTU statement in 1953, that he wrote personally to this effect to the ICFTU headquarters in Brussels. He arranged for Bill and Gordon to meet the Assistant General Secretary of the ICFTU, Alfred Brauntahl, in Brussels.

After their discussion Brauntahl said, 'The ICFTU never meant to condemn MRA.'

In August, 1966, in an official press release, the ICFTU said that they had 'an attitude of strict neutrality' to MRA.

Since then there has been the closest understanding between the ICFTU and MRA. Bill Jordan, the first British General Secretary of the ICFTU, which has 91 million members, is a man for whom Bill Jaeger has the highest regard.

*　　*　　*　　*　　*

112

Ever since arriving in the USA Bill had realised how strong the current climate of anti-Communism was. The sure-fire way to reach agreement with most Americans was to trot out the anti-Communist 'line'. Communism was the enemy, and must be contained at all costs, and the United States, now the most powerful democratic nation in the world, tried hard to block the expansion of this dangerous idea.

It may also be accurate to say that some of the strong anti-Communist thinking so prevalent in the USA was absorbed, if only subconsciously, into Bill's own thinking during those American years, and may have influenced his judgment. This was perhaps understandable, since the work of MRA had often suffered from misinformation and attacks published by the Soviet press.

Bill had had dealings with Communists all his life, and had always sought to offer an idea bigger than Communism, one that would include every class, every race, every religion. He was always interested to study the thinking and writing that emerged from Communists all over the world. He felt society did need to change, but believed that using divisive methods would hinder and not help. Social justice involved more than economics or new systems.

One Washington body especially concerned with Communist infiltration was the FBI, under J Edgar Hoover.

One day Bill received a phone call from an FBI man, asking if he would come to the Bureau's headquarters for a meeting. This man, an assistant director under Hoover, mentioned the name of a professor in California, a friend of Bill's, who had suggested the meeting.

Bill welcomed this chance to discuss his work. He gave a survey of the industrial situation in Britain and Europe and facts about the work of MRA with the unions. He explained the aims and personnel of those working with Moral Re-Armament, and clarified the point that it was not a sect or some impractical religious group.

Bill kept in touch with the assistant director regularly, and the man said some years later: 'Anybody can attack

113

MRA, but if we hear of a particularly virulent attack in a certain situation, we feel there may be a need for us to look into the validity of it, and the motivation behind it. MRA acts as a kind of litmus paper.'

X

Washington with hindsight

The nine years Bill spent in America from 1953 to 1962 were probably the most decisive of his life. He was to look back on them some years later as a time when he gained far-reaching insights about human nature, including his own – lessons it had been essential to learn.

There was no doubt that Bill's deepest feelings involved his wife and his son. He enjoyed the dimension that fatherhood brought to his life. He loved to surprise us, and to give us things: with me it was flowers or books; with Fred it could be going to the movies, or to a bowling alley, out to a special meal, a baseball game, and playing chess.

Each summer after the school term was over we had a month's holiday away together at a family resort where there would be swimming, boating and tennis.

Fred enjoyed his school life and did well in his work, each year winning the prize for best scholar in his class. Eventually he became Head of the Lower School. He had many good friends at school and often spent the weekend in their homes.

But, perhaps like many other husbands and fathers, Bill had not really worked out how to combine a busy life, often travelling away from home, with giving thought to the quality of time that he spent with his wife and son.

*   *   *   *   *

Ever since the creation of the wartime revue *You Can De-fend America*, it had become clear that one of the quickest ways to spread the message of MRA was through stage shows, both musicals and straight plays. The decade of the fifties was a richly creative period for these productions. Peter Howard, former journalist on the London *Daily Express*, had worked with Buchman since 1940 and had used his talented pen to write many books, articles and stage plays ever since. In 1954 he and others created *The Vanishing Island*, dramatising the divide in the world between the democracies and the dictatorships.

The musical show had been honed and polished in Hollywood. Several well-known actors were in the large cast, the music was superb, and its theme was both universal and timely.

To accompany the show there was to be a group of distinguished speakers from all walks of life, among them William Grogan, International Vice-President of the Transport Workers Union, and his wife Molly. Grogan was a long-standing friend and colleague of Bill's, from his work with the American unions.

In Bill's mind, he just took it for granted that he would be part of the group travelling around the world with *The Vanishing Island*. But for me the decision was not clear-cut. Fred was only eight years old at the time and I was torn in two by realising on the one hand how hard it would be for Fred to understand and cope with a long separation, and a feeling that I ought to go, that other colleagues expected me to accompany Bill.

Anxiety for the good opinion of my colleagues won out and I went, though with a heavy heart. We were eventually away from Fred for 18 months, as after Asia the show went on to tour Europe. It was a deeply moving moment when I finally met up again with the little boy who had been brought to the small local airport to meet me, and who stood alone on the tarmac, so quietly, waiting for his mother.

Fred was looked after as a son by the Vondermuhlls and

other friends during that time, but with hindsight it was a wrong decision on my part, made from the wrong motives.

* * * * *

Of course our family's experience was not unique. Many families in all walks of life are expected to accommodate themselves to the needs and conditions of a particular job, and have to take upheavals in their stride.

What is it like for children who have parents dedicated to a cause? Does 'the cause' come first? Are the children automatically expected to take up the same dedicated life? If they don't, do they bring distress to the parents? What should the parents' attitude be in this situation?

For any child the early teenage years can be difficult enough without additional pressures being even unintentionally added by his parents. Especially if he loves his parents, it makes it harder for him to be a free agent and to sort out what his own beliefs and direction in life are to be.

In our case, we didn't handle it well. In the back of our minds at that time we hoped and almost took for granted that our son would follow in our footsteps and take up a life dedicated to the aims and principles of MRA. Even without saying anything, we released a strong current of control around him. As Fred reached his teenage years it began to dawn on us that he was not especially interested in the life we were involved in.

There were several developments in the work of MRA which brought an additional element of confusion and uncertainty into our lives.

* * * * *

In a strange way, simultaneously with all the activity and creativity in the late 1950s, a kind of zealotry came into being. In the mistaken belief that they were acting responsibly, people freely pointed out any shortcomings their colleagues might have.

117

An inordinate number of long letters went back and forth, highlighting places where individuals might be off the track and needed to do better. Because some people became self-righteous and judgmental, others became fearful and inward looking.

Bill received a letter like this, more or less implying that the labour work might be getting off the track. When I read the letter I began to feel panic. I hadn't realised how much my security was in my husband's success.

I put the brakes on Bill as a result of that criticism, cautioning him to be careful. I didn't question what was said. If friends suggested Bill was moving in the wrong direction, then I too-readily assumed they must be right.

Bill had always been rocklike in his resolve and had a marked objectivity in his approach to the ups and downs of life. Soon after our marriage Bill had recognised that I did not know how self-centred I was, the immaturity which meant that I was too partisan in my reactions and so missed the truth. He had not found it easy when I had burst forth at times, but so far he had not let these outbursts drive him off course.

However, he found it difficult to handle my latest reactions over the implied criticism sent him by letter, since his own work was involved. And as Bill said, 'If you build up a work, you want to defend it.' About this time an uncertainty began to come into his life, concern at what some of his colleagues might be thinking about his work, most especially Buchman.

*   *   *   *   *

After *The Vanishing Island*, several more musical shows were created and drew large audiences. Bill often travelled with them, while I mostly remained at home with Fred.

Bill came back to Washington in the summer of 1959.

Dinner parties and receptions were frequent events in the home which served as headquarters for MRA in

118

Washington, and there was a group of Washington host-esses in the diplomatic and military circles who arranged occasions to hear about MRA's work. Bill had in the past often been called on to speak at these occasions.

That summer, after hearing Bill speak, a Washington hostess arranged for him to meet her husband, an admiral in the navy. The admiral was interested in what Bill had to say and in his diagnosis of the ideological issues at work in the world, and the need to be able to 'read men', as Bill put it.

Then another senior admiral sent word through his wife, who knew the wife of the first admiral, that he too would be interested in meeting Bill. And in the next weeks some of the army and airforce personnel also said they would like to hear what Bill had to say.

Most of those normally resident at the Washington MRA headquarters where this entertaining took place were away at the Michigan summer conference. When someone suggested Bill and I should move into the head-quarters and really take charge, we did so.

Throughout those summer months in 1959 Bill and I were caught up in what might be called a social whirl, as the new friends in the military invited us to their homes, and we in turn laid on dinners and receptions for them.

As hostess in the MRA headquarters I was in charge, at first reluctantly, and then as the entertaining appeared to be a success, the position went to my head.

Bill began to realise that he now had the ear of an im-portant group concerned with American security. As al-ways, he looked for a team to work with him, and he soon found the ideal one. He first enlisted a recent arrival to the city, Rajmohan Gandhi, grandson of Mahatma Gandhi. Rajmohan's father, editor of the *Hindustan Times* in India, had known Frank Buchman well, and young Gandhi had run into MRA while working as a journalist in Edinburgh, and came to Washington at the invitation of Buchman. Another man Bill enlisted on his calls to the military was Dr Douglas Cornell, Executive Officer of the National

119

Academy of Sciences. He was a near neighbour of ours, and his son was a friend of Fred's.

The same kind of briefings also took place in the Pentagon and helped to clarify for the American military and security forces the aims and purposes of MRA, so that in the future they were able to give an unqualified certificate of approval to MRA's work.

* * * * *

That autumn the headquarters filled up again as many returned from the summer conference. It is difficult to explain how we could have made a mistake like that, but Bill and I continued to stay on there, persuading ourselves that we were needed, while Fred lived at the Vondermuhlls' across town, and continued his schooling.

This arrangement demonstrated how our sense of the necessity of the work we were engaged in caused us to do what in hindsight is hard to understand. It was not apparent to us at the time, as it seemed in keeping with the general atmosphere of urgency about MRA's work and important role in world affairs.

Broadly speaking, a rigidity of thinking had developed in the mentality of us all which led, quite naturally, to a loss of balanced judgment. We sincerely believed we had a huge task, demanding sacrifices akin to those of wartime, and there was no way that personal wishes could take priority.

Eventually one of our wiser friends suggested Bill and I should take our son away on a family holiday. This we did, returning to the family summer resort we had often used before. We all enjoyed the swimming, boating and tennis and the mountain air, but there was a shyness in both of us which kept our conversation on a safe non-personal level. Yet the time together enabled us to re-establish a family life.

* * * * *

The decade of the fifties drew to a close. Buchman died in the summer of 1961. Peter Howard, his natural successor, stepped into the role of leadership of MRA.

Howard always made clear that he respected Bill's commitment and valued the way Bill had built up MRA's industrial work. He and Bill had often exchanged letters and ever since our unfortunate summer of 1959 in Washington he had written to Bill and myself to encourage us in our family life.

We in turn tried to keep him up to date with our hopes and our anxieties.

In the summer of 1962 we received a letter from him, wondering if it might be time for the Jaeger family to move back to England. Perhaps, Howard suggested, since Fred had been born in England, he should finish his education in an English school. Equally, Bill could take up his work again in the European labour field, including the ILO, and try to resolve the confusion over the ICFTU report.

This idea we found extremely shaking at first. Were we being moved out of America – not wanted there any more? And what would it mean to Fred, being suddenly uprooted at a crucial stage of his schooling?

Bill and I had very little sleep that night, as we discussed the suggestion. Then gradually, towards daybreak, we both began to feel that perhaps it was a good idea after all. A good English school might be helpful to Fred, at a stage when teenage partying with friends seemed to have a higher priority than studying.

We sent a message back to Howard accepting his suggestion, and when we heard that an English headmaster Bill knew was willing to take Fred into his school, that seemed to put the seal on it. We both began to sense a rightness about this next step in our lives.

And so mid-December, 1962, saw Bill, his wife and his son on board the BOAC night flight to London.

*   *   *   *   *

121

The grammar school which accepted Fred was in Cornwall, so that was where we headed. Bill based in London, where he picked up his work as Howard had suggested. He would come down as often as he could on the overnight train to Penzance, then a bus ride and a walk along the cliff to the little cottage we had taken. Its remoteness from the busy, sophisticated life of Washington gave us a chance to gain perspective and Cornwall's wild and often storm-lashed beauty cleared away some of the cobwebs in our thinking.

Bill and I talked long and deep. Being in that remote situation seemed to emphasise that we were meant to sort ourselves out, perhaps to make a new beginning.

We discussed the amount of time we had been away from Fred, quite often at the wrong times, and recognised how we had really put 'the cause' first, before our son. So much of our motivation came back to what people would have thought of us, especially our friends and Buchman himself.

As my mind cleared, I began to see the incongruity of almost demanding that our son accept a vocation in MRA at that time, when I was lost and unhappy in it myself. I asked him one day if he had found me difficult. His reply was that I talked so often in a moralising jargon.

This cleared the air between us and made me see more clearly that I had often made it difficult for Bill by my emotional outbursts, and how he had had to make his way in spite of them.

'You have a wrong sense of guilt,' Bill said during one of our talks. And then he said, 'Many people find it hard to understand how anyone from the British working class really feels – a person from that background always feels inferior and insecure.'

We faced the fact that we had somehow gotten off the track during those final years in Washington.

'Never to lose my vision,' Bill said when reflecting on this time. He realised the importance of retaining an inner calm. 'There is need for silence, especially when things are not easy.'

In all life's ups and downs, he never went back on his calling to do something for other people.

It seemed to be a turning point for both of us, and we began to feel more and more sure that it was a positive step, as we noticed that Fred was responding to his English schooling.

The school opened doors for Fred into the realms of literature, history, poetry and eventually philosophy. His interest in music began to move from Ray Charles to Beethoven, Mozart and Wagner – especially Wagner. During a trip to London the family went together to Covent Garden Opera House to hear Parsifal, and though the seats were in the gods, hard and wooden, and looked down from what seemed a vast height, we sat transported.

In 1964 we left Cornwall, and Fred finished his schooling closer to London. From there it was three years at Southampton University for a BA and then a B Phil from Oxford.

Our attitudes toward our son quite changed. We let him go. He felt this loosening of control, and responded by seeking us out, not all at once, but bit by bit.

XI

The people's lifeboat at the ILO

1963

Bill's heart lifted when, back in Europe, he was able to attend the ILO conference held every June in Geneva.

For the next 30 years he would be at the ILO every year in June, and often in November and February as well, when the Governing Body met.

As mentioned earlier, the ILO was set up in 1919 to bring governments, employers and trade unionists together for united action in the cause of social justice and better conditions of work everywhere. ILO Conventions cover a wide field of social problems, including basic human rights, minimum wages, working conditions, social security, occupational safety and health.

At its inception in 1919 the ILO comprised 42 member states. In 1992 the number of countries represented there had grown to 173.

David Morse, ILO Director-General for 22 years, said: 'The world is now too small, the danger to peace is already too great, to enable us to tolerate any longer flagrant inequalities among men. We are shocked at the cynicism of man towards his neighbours. We can no longer afford to let our world economy run blind as though no moral or social implications are involved.'

Bill often quotes from one of his speeches: 'We need to bring about material advances, but even when we do, it is only one side of the coin. The other half is men's motives and attitudes and how to change them. Material development is a false god unless there runs parallel with it a spiritual and ethical development that enables man to accept and live at peace with his neighbour.'

Bill attended the ILO conference as Press, representing a British labour paper, *The Industrial Pioneer*.

It was not long before colleagues who had worked with him through the years joined him each June in Geneva. Chief of these was Duncan Corcoran, whose eyes, like Bill's would light up as he moved among the thousand or so delegates, on the lookout for former friends and alert to make new ones.

Two Swiss, Daniel Mottu and François Maunoir, formed the basis of a year-long presence among the ILO delegates in Geneva. They both had many natural contacts, and both had worked extensively in Latin America. Bill had met Mottu first at the 1948 ILO conference in San Francisco.

The Swiss MRA office in Geneva was not far from the Palais des Nations, and comprised a suite of rooms including a small kitchen, where meals could be served, or small receptions held for guests from the ILO, and daily planning meetings could take place for Bill and those who spent long hours at the conference.

*   *   *   *   *

The ILO conference building is a vast place with a full-time staff of over 800, where many languages are spoken.

Delegates, naturally absorbed in their own particular interests, move primarily among their own group. Year in, year out, Bill's simple ways of meeting people remained unchanged. He would, for instance, go up and talk to people after they had spoken from the platform, to make some

126

encouraging remark to them, and very often he would follow up this initial contact with a letter or even an enclosure of some printed matter which he believed would inform and interest them.

He would meet people in the corridors, in the cafeteria, in the lift between floors; apart from attending and listening in on the plenary sessions, there were many hours of walking around the huge building, and simply waiting around for the right moment to approach and speak to anyone he and his team felt they should get to know.

Peter Sutcliffe, British Press Officer at the ILO, described Bill's work there:

'It has happened so often, for so long, that it has become a standard feature of working procedure. I emerge from my office bent on yet one more burdensome errand, weighed with the cares of the hour, and there approaching me, in silhouette against the corridor lighting, is the unmistakable form of Bill Jaeger. He is once again visiting the ILO, to keep himself up to date on our work on human rights and international relations, and to keep us up to date on his.

'No stormbound sailor welcomed more warmly the arrival of a Trinity House lifeboat than I greet that of Bill in the ILO. Come to think of it, he even looks a bit like a lifeboat, rolling and bobbing with the surge of the tide, butting into the wind, powering his sturdy timbers ever forward as if under the impulse of 5,000 hp twin Perkins diesels. Always on course. Always arriving.

'And what cheer he brings. Since we last met three months before those twin diesels have taken him to Central America or Eastern Europe or China, or all three, and from all corners of the globe he brings tidings of unquenchable hope in the triumph of the human spirit. That beaming smile under those quiet, friendly eyes banishes one's paltry preoccupations, lifting one's sights from the surrounding waters to the ocean's level, sunlit horizon. In a few moments – for he merely heaves to alongside, engines turning over, never making fast – he has saluted the quarter-deck, transhipped his cargo, taken on mine and logged a course bearing for the next voyage. Then he signals full ahead on the engine-room telegraph and heads off into the wind. How calm are the seas in his wake.

'The lifeboat has been entering ILO territorial waters now for well over half a century. Much has changed in that time in the political and human environment in which we both navigate. Perhaps each of us, and both of us together, may have helped that change take place for, as a delegate remarked to an ILO debate here, "We are here not to be polite, but to make a difference."

'Sail on Bill ... do continue to make a difference.'

* * * * *

In 1965 Bill met the National President of the Wood Industry Employers of Czechoslovakia. He was a close friend of Alexander Dubcek, the Prime Minister. He had heard of the work of Caux, and while attending an ILO conference in Geneva he invited Bill and a Swiss colleague, Heinrich Karrer, to visit the furniture factory of which he was General Manager, employing 2,000 workers, in Prievidza.

Bill and Heini took up the invitation, and had meetings in the factory with the workers' leaders. At the end of a two-hour discussion on industrial issues, the chairman of the workers' council invited Bill and Heini to his home for lunch, along with a number of convinced Communist Party members, and the General Manager.

At the end of the lunch the General Manager said, 'In the light of our discussions about Caux and MRA, I want to ask you three questions. First, do I have to believe in God?'

Bill replied, 'I do, but whether you do is up to you. What matters is that you listen to your conscience and obey it, call it what you like.'

The second question was, 'Is MRA the next step in history for the Communist world as well as the non-Communist world?' Bill replied that was what he believed.

20 Caux, Switzerland, the MRA centre for reconciliation and reconstruction established by the Swiss in 1946

22 Paul Kurowski and Max Bladek, German miners, Marxist theorists, and communist leaders from Moers

Devastation in the Ruhr, Germany, 1948

MRA speakers address management and miner's leaders from 150 Ruhr pits.

24 In 1953 John Riffe was standing for election to the executive vice-presidency of the CIO. The Jaegers moved to the USA to support him.

25 Fred Small, longshoreman from Brooklyn: 'Bill Jaeger – you can tell him anything, his advice is always good. I'm just glad he is my friend.'

26 Fred Jaeger and his father at a game of chess

27 The lakeside setting of the International Labour Organisation (ILO) headquarters in Geneva. It stands in the background, to the right, with the UN buildings in the foreground. (*From a painting by Peter Sutcliffe*)

28 Bill Jaeger has attended the ILO conferences for over 50 years. Peter Sutcliffe (right), British Press Officer, comments: 'From all quarters of the globe he brings tidings of unquenchable hope in the triumph of the human spirit.'

29 Meeting the Minister of Labour of Senegal, President of the ILO in 1951

30 At the MRA conference, Caux, 1953. Bill Jaeger with Sibnath Banerjee and his wife. Banerjee was President of the Indian National TUC, the Hind Mazdoor Sabha.

31 Eduard Rozental (left), Novosti Press Representative in Geneva, breakfasti with Bill and Clara Jaeger and a Novosti colleague at the Caux Conferen 1960. 'In spite of differences,' he said, 'all of us – Soviet, English, Swiss, Fren American, Brazilian and other participants in this conference – have found common language on the basis of generally accepted values which have boundary.'

The third question came quickly, 'You mean then that your idea is a kind of detector of truth for mankind. Is that what you mean?'

Some time later the General Manager sent a delegation of workers to a conference at Caux where industry was the focus. They arrived on the day the Russian army invaded Czechoslovakia. The delegation was led by the chairman of shop stewards and by the Party agent in charge of security. They were all astonished at the freedom and openness of Caux and the people they met there.

Bill and Karrer returned three times in later years to visit them in their homes in Prievidza, where the chairman of shop stewards told them that he had been training 50 of his colleagues in the factory in what he himself had learnt at Caux.

*   *   *   *   *

In June, 1969, Bill received an invitation from the President of the Arab Confederation of Trade Unionists, who was the Workers' delegate to the ILO, to visit Egypt and Jordan, and to bring with him a delegation of British trade unionists.

Bill gathered a group from the British docks, from the aircraft industry, and from the car industry. He also asked a colleague of his, William Conner, to join the delegation. Conner had served in the desert war in 1942, and had maintained his links and friendships with people there ever since.

The delegation was royally received in Cairo. Hours were spent in discussion with their hosts. For the Arabs it was an eye-opener when, for the first time in their lives, they heard Englishmen speak honestly about where they had been wrong in their attitudes toward the Arab world, and then give examples of where they themselves needed to change.

In Jordan the British delegation met the trade union federation, who took them on a tour of the vast Baqa

Palestinian Refugee camp, where 20,000 lived in great squalor on a daily handout of United Nations grain. Having seen what it was like for these seemingly abandoned people, Bill and his party had a greater understanding of why the Arabs felt as they did.

Then came a delicate matter: would they like to meet some people of the newly formed El Fatah movement, later to become the core group of the PLO (Palestine Liberation Organisation). There was only a slight hesitation before they agreed to the meeting.

The party was taken to the outskirts of Amman, where they met with 30 from El Fatah. Outstanding among the men they met was Khalid Al Hassan, later to become probably the most effective negotiator of the PLO. From that first meeting, contact was maintained with him, though not without difficulty at times. In 1980 he and his wife spent 12 days at the Caux summer conference.

He, more than anybody, was credited with the change that took place in PLO policy between 1975 and 1985 which culminated in Yasser Arafat's renunciation of violence from the rostrum of the United Nations in Geneva in 1988, and from which began the first serious Middle East peace process.

After returning to Britain Bill Conner kept in contact with Al Hassan, and maintained his friendships with the Arab world.

*   *   *   *   *

As well as the yearly attendance at the ILO in Geneva, Bill liked to be present at the conferences in Britain of the TUC, the Labour party and the Conservative party. He never missed a year, after his return to Europe. As well as the large plenary sessions, what Bill enjoyed was looking in on some of the many fringe meetings taking place, because they helped him discover some of the things being discussed which were not always reported in the press.

During the Labour party conference one year, Bill went

to a fringe meeting of about 100 put on by the Young Trotskyites to discuss unemployment. At the interval Bill went forward and spoke to the young woman who was chairing the meeting, telling her he appreciated the passion and sincerity with which she and the other speakers had presented the subject. He told her he was from the north of England, and had known poverty in his youth.

She asked if he would be willing to speak at the end of the meeting, which he did. He told of his background, and how he had given his life to create a better social order, and quoted Frank Buchman: 'There's enough in the world for everyone's need, but not enough for everyone's greed.' Bill suggested to his listeners that they could take on the same big task in the world that he had done.

At the end, when he finished, several came forward to thank him. One said, 'We never hear things like this.'

Kumar Raval, a young British law student, first met Bill at a fringe meeting of the Labour party. Kumar was speaking as a representative of Asian youth in Britain.

'I was really nervous when I spoke. It was the anniversary of Mahatma Gandhi's birth, and I spoke, among other things, about our local Hindu temple, which was being threatened with closure.

'I was by far the youngest on the platform, and the audience included many senior figures, but at the end I got a standing ovation, led by Bill who simply stood up and applauded, looking round until others rose and applauded also.

'Afterwards Bill marched towards the dais where I was talking to someone, waited patiently until the conversation was over, then climbed up on the dais and put both his hands on my shoulders, this burly chap, and literally shook me, saying, "Well done." He offered me a good deal of encouragement, and then he said – and this was what caught my interest – "I know Gandhi's grandson, you know; I'll give you his address."

'Bill gave me his card – it said 'MRA' on it and I was a

131

bit suspicious as to what that meant. He offered me his pen and notebook, to write my name and address. I returned the book to him and was absent-mindedly about to pocket the pen, when he reminded me that it was his! That was sharp of him. There was a lot else going on around us, and many other people would not have realised about the pen, but he did, with a smile.

'He got in touch with me later, and he persisted even though I was not initially responsive. He could have just said "hello" to me then in Brighton, but he didn't; he picked me out and my life has changed ever since.

'He sees the potential in everyone. He treats everyone the same. I have seen him at the ILO greeting the ministers and dignitaries in exactly the same genuinely friendly way as he greeted me, a young student, when we first met.'

*   *   *   *   *

Bill and I went to South Africa in the latter part of 1976. Our host was an old friend of Bill's, Bremer Hofmeyr, from a prominent Afrikaner family. He and Bill had worked together in America in the war years.

Many receptions and meetings were arranged during our visit, and we met white businessmen, as well as black and coloured South Africans who were friends of the Hofmeyrs. MRA's programme in South Africa, as anywhere in the world, had consistently sought to break down the barriers between people, whether of race, colour or religion.

Bill said to his hosts that he would very much like to meet people from the black trade unions, organisations which were in their early stages of development. Previously the unions had been mostly white.

This was arranged, and Bill and I went to their headquarters, where we made the acquaintance of one of the leading black women in the Garment Workers' Union. She unburdened herself to us about the difficult situation they were in, and all the problems besetting them as they tried to establish their union.

132

The ILO, by this time, had decided to allow black delegates to attend the annual conferences in Geneva as observers. This was something which seemed, to the ILO, to be a step forward.

But Bill, as he moved around the ILO conference the following year, came upon the black trade union lady and her group, and found her clearly very unhappy. No one from Africa would speak to her, she said, even though she was black, because she came from South Africa.

Bill realised how she was saddened by the ideological prejudice that cut people off – even those who were the victims of apartheid themselves. The stigma of being a South African in those days applied equally to those who were bravely fighting for the rights of their people.

Bill and his team took her under their wing, had meals with her, introduced her to other friends of theirs, and took her, with a large party of ILO delegates, up to Caux for a day visit.

Making his way around the milling throngs in the corridors of the ILO building at about the same time, Bill came upon a group of black delegates talking together rather heatedly, obviously upset about something. One figure stood out from the others, a very large Zulu. The radio news earlier that morning had carried the story about several hundred people being shot in Soweto.

Bill approached the group, and said he was sorry for what had happened.

'Who are you?' demanded the large man belligerently.

Bill introduced himself, and said he had been working for many years with international labour in the work of Moral Re-Armament.

That was the end of the conversation, but Bill wrote to the man several times over the following months. A year later, at the ILO once again, the tall Zulu sought Bill out, and asked if they could have lunch together.

Over the meal he asked Bill, 'Can you help me with my young men? They only want to kill each other.' Bill talked to him from his own experiences of helping people who are frustrated and bitter, and invited him to visit Caux, where he could meet others committed to the work of MRA, and perhaps find new ways of approaching his problem.

The Zulu went to Caux with a group of others from the ILO and, having listened to speakers at a meeting there and talked at length with his hosts, he was very thoughtful on the return journey to Geneva.

Over the next years this man came to regard Bill as a real friend, every year bringing fresh people to meet him. Bill said to him once, 'The next ten years are meant to be the best years of your life.'

'Why?' asked the big man.

'Because you are meant to unite the best black people and the best white people in your country.'

'Never, if it means compromise,' came the reply.

'That's what both the white and the blacks say,' responded Bill. 'What is needed is for both to take on the rebuilding of South Africa.' And that was what the man did, and became a truly constructive force in the country.

*   *   *   *   *

Bill made five visits to South America. On one of them, in 1984, he visited Argentina after the war in the Falklands. As an Englishman he was able to apologise for the years of closed hearts and minds England had shown towards Argentine feelings.

He went on to Chile and Uruguay, and after giving an address to the Uruguayan Congress of Labour, the whole committee signed a letter of thanks to him for his lifelong commitment to world labour, and for what it had meant to them and to other nations.

In 1985 Luis Alberto Monge was elected President of Costa Rica. As a young man in 1948 he had attended the ILO conference in San Francisco, at which time he met Bill and Daniel Mottu.

134

After taking office in 1985 Monge sent a message to Mottu, 'I am awaiting the teams of MRA in my country.' He publicly attributed the change to democratic progress in Costa Rica, from years of violence and military coups, to conferences which took place in Caux between the young men like himself who 'wanted to change things'.

Following his message, the new President arranged a special meeting with some of the cabinet in San Jose, which Bill and Mottu attended.

* * * * *

To mark the 50th anniversary in 1994 of the ILO conference in Philadelphia in 1944, the editor of the ILO magazine, *World of Work,* Michel Fromont, asked Bill to write a piece for publication.

By way of introduction, Fromont said, 'There are few witnesses or actors in the ILO's history who can pretend to go as far as Bill Jaeger: 82 years of age, bright and lively, and ever assiduous during meetings of the Governing Body and the International Labour Conference.'

The article was entitled: 'I was in Philadelphia...' , and in it Bill wrote,

'I was present at the historic 26th Conference of the ILO in Philadelphia in 1944, and was deeply moved by the statement in the famous Declaration issued then to the world for the first time:

'"All human beings, irrespective of race, creed or sex, have the right to pursue both their material well-being and their spiritual development in conditions of freedom and dignity, of economic security and equal opportunity."'

* * * * *

Because of their patient, sensitive approach, Bill, Mottu, Corcoran and their team made countless friends over the years. One who became a real ally was P P Narayanan, an Indian from Malaysia. Bill and his friends met him first in

1953, as a young man and president of the Malaysian TUC, and workers' delegate to the ILO. A warm friendship developed and they met regularly for the next 38 years, by which time Narayanan had become head of 91 million workers, when he was elected President of the ICFTU.

Meeting Frank Buchman, Narayanan once said, was the turning point of his life. He also said that he had learnt two important things in the course of his meetings with Bill and his colleagues at the ILO. For a man whose life was involved in delicate, sometimes difficult, negotiations, he said it was vital to realise two things: 'I don't have to hate the man I disagree with,' and 'Every saint has a past, and every sinner has a future.'

XII

Conflict and a new beginning

Is there anything to compare with the intensity of feeling that exists between friends and comrades of a sacrificial, dedicated cause who, through some turn of events, find themselves on opposite sides, each holding passionate convictions that their side is right and the others wrong?

History has tragically shown that religious beliefs focus this more than most. Civil wars have been fought to promote or defend a cause. Families have been painfully divided, brother against brother, parents against children.

In the spring of 1966 Bill found himself becoming involved in just such a difficult situation, among friends and former colleagues in MRA. It would occupy many of his waking hours for the next ten years.

For the USA and Europe, the sixties were traumatic. The assassination of John Kennedy, race riots in major American cities, the Vietnam war and 'make love not war' – these were the rites of passage of a generation who began to experiment with new lifestyles, often turning against traditional values.

But hand in hand with the negative side there was also a certain optimism abroad in 'the sixties generation'. They were the ones who were going to save the world, to change the world, to feed, clothe and house the world within a decade perhaps – certainly in their own lifetimes. But first it would be necessary to reject the ways of the older generation.

How could the imagination and restless energy of the rebellious young become a fully creative and constructive force? Peter Howard, the Englishman who succeeded to the world leadership of MRA after Frank Buchman's death in 1961, toured American universities in 1964, challenging students to build 'The Great Society', starting in their own lives.

Hundreds responded, and came to MRA conferences on Mackinac Island, Michigan. Inspired by Howard and others, and with the talented composers and musicians who had produced Howard's last show, *Space Is So Startling*, the young Americans produced a brilliant new show, *Sing-Out*, that spoke directly to the high-school and college generation of America.

Its theme song was *Up With People*, and the whole show – a collection of songs and sketches – had tremendous energy and pace, and an almost irresistible rhythm and beat.

But just at that time, during a strenuous trip to South America in 1965, Peter Howard died of viral pneumonia. Because of a tireless commitment to countless individuals who sought his counselling and advice after Buchman's death, and the recent whirlwind series of speaking engagements in American universities, he had seriously overtaxed his strength. He died at the premature age of 57, only four years after Buchman himself.

His sudden death left a leadership crisis for MRA. There was no one obvious candidate to follow him, though people in both America and Britain, either collectively or individually, sought to give leadership and direction to MRA's global work.

The show whose concept Howard had inspired was launched in Washington, DC, in June, 1965. The sight of a stage filled with 200 young men and women, singing and dancing to inspired music and lyrics, touched the hearts of the sophisticated audience. At the end, in response to the theme song, they rose and joined in with the cast on the stage by singing and clapping.

*   *   *   *   *

In the next months, and following extensive tours with the show, an explosion of productions of *Sing-Out* took place in the USA. Casts sprang up also in many parts of Europe, and as far away as South Africa, South America and Australia. Bill and several other colleagues attended performances. It was undoubtedly a superb show, but the moral and spiritual content of the original production had been superseded by a more specifically patriotic and educational theme. The success of the show itself seemed to be the chief objective.

This very rapid expansion and popularity, coupled with the evident change of emphasis, created unease among many older colleagues of Buchman and Howard, especially in Britain. It was feared that some of MRA's most basic and universal foundations were being eroded. After many years of not infrequent attacks and misinformation about MRA, suddenly there was spectacular success and popularity for this show. Perhaps, some said, Buchman's concepts of a life wholly given to God, of seeking to live by absolute moral standards – which had never been easy and often attracted criticism – were being set aside in favour of a less difficult and more popular lifestyle.

An English colleague of Bill's went to the USA and attempted to discuss the growing division with his American counterpart. Unfortunately the visit did more harm than good, since hurtful words were exchanged by both men, and they parted amid deep mistrust.

In May, 1966, the Englishman told Bill and a few others in London that his information was that *Sing-Out* was being put forward by the Americans as the next step in MRA's development, just as MRA had developed from the Oxford Group. He regarded this as a matter which should be strenuously opposed.

So developed a struggle for control over the direction that would be taken, with damaging effects on all sides. In the following months, all over the world, the international body of MRA began to divide into two camps: those wanting to go along with *Sing-Out*, and those wanting to preserve MRA. Communications between the two camps broke down, and misunderstandings flourished. Bill found himself travelling to many countries to reassure people and protect the MRA parent body.

At Easter in 1968, Bill's London colleague wrote a strongly worded article criticising those who dismissed MRA as 'a rigid rule', and who measured their own success by the extent of popular support. The article was printed and circulated among people interested in MRA's work around the world.

The gap steadily widened and deepened between former friends and colleagues on each side of the argument.

Bill did not agree with all that was being said and done in London any more than he agreed with the methods and motivations of those organising *Sing-Out*. 'I did not believe it was right to go along with the thing which was not the basic way of life of MRA, as I saw it. But I also did not feel it was right to turn against anyone. In a situation like that you have to try and keep the spirit yourself.'

*　　*　　*　　*　　*

In 1968 *Sing-Out* changed its name to *Up With People,* and incorporated itself separately, though Moral Re-Armament in America continued to support them financially and in other ways. The show grew in popularity, with young people queuing up to join it.

Meanwhile, Caux continued to provide a uniting focus for MRA worldwide. Each summer delegates came from all corners of the globe and from every kind of background, just as they had done for over 20 years. In 1970 people were there from 23 countries, about 700 in all.

It was during this summer, in mid-August, that *The New York Times* published a long article announcing that Moral Re-Armament was sharply curtailing its US operations, and selling its valuable US offices and training centres, many of which had been donated to Buchman for his work by their owners in the forties and fifties. The article gave a brief history of Buchman's life and work, and indicated that MRA continued unabated in Europe and other parts of the world, but that in the USA it was seen as a religious movement, affiliation with which was a handicap to *Up With People*, hence the dissociation. The article said MRA had 'seen its day', and quoted several well-known and often repudiated criticisms.

At Caux a small group met privately to see what response could be made. A statement was drawn up, showing how MRA was indeed still effectively at work, and signed by the executive secretaries of 18 MRA legal bodies in countries around the world.

The plan was to hand-deliver the statement to the paper in New York, for publication as soon as possible. Three men were to take it: Mitchell Bingham, son of an American senator, and one of the many Americans who wanted to support and maintain MRA as it was originally conceived; Dr Paul Campbell, a Canadian who had been Frank Buchman's physician for many years and who had known the Americans in charge of *Up With People*; and Bill. The three flew off to New York immediately.

The New York Times never published the statement, and when approached a second time by the three men, they said it was no longer news. This was a disappointment, but there was another way forward.

Bill, Campbell and Bingham decided to look up as many old friends as they could and seek chances to talk together face to face – something which had not been done in any meaningful way over the previous months and years.

When people heard they were around, many invitations began to come in.

In the next three years there were hundreds of such meetings. Bill, Campbell and Bingham and a number of others were able to spend time with the local MRA groups and individual supporters in different parts of the North American continent, many of whom didn't know what the acrimony was all about.

Many found it almost impossible to understand how people who had previously dedicated themselves to a concept like MRA could ever fall out with each other. It was a contradiction of the message they were preaching to the world, and it was painful to accept. Bill and his colleagues also gave the matter much thought, as they tried to understand the situation.

Initially Bill had assumed that he and those remaining faithful to the MRA parent body were in the right, and the others were wrong. But gradually, as he talked to more and more people, he began to understand why so many of his old friends had welcomed *Up With People*, giving it the support they had once given to MRA.

There had been the unhappy period in the late fifties, when MRA had been too inward-looking and many people had been seriously hurt. Quite simply, *Up With People* provided a breath of fresh air, and a relief from a pressure to conform.

It also seemed to Bill that one of the causes of the division was the relationship which often exists between leaders and followers.

Some like to be led. It relieves them from responsibility. Some follow directives because they want the good opinion of the leader. Some follow because they find it difficult to speak up against someone who has an aura of authority. Some follow because they think such people know best and it is right to do as they say. Some follow because they fear that if they don't do so they will be in the doghouse. The same tendencies equally apply in politics, or in business, or in the world of trade unions.

The 20th century had seen the rise of powerful and divisive ideologies, in each case initiated by the ability of one individual to sway large audiences by his use of words.

At the same time, prophet voices and inspiring leadership have always been needed in the world, to raise the sights and the hopes of people.

What is it that happens between leaders and followers? In the case of charismatic, convincing orators, the arguments put forth can be so persuasive that the listening followers can find themselves carried away by forceful presentation. The majority accept what is being said, and the few who do not are tempted to keep quiet.

Bill was familiar with speakers of this kind on both sides of the Atlantic where leadership was being given, in MRA and in *Up With People*. Yet Buchman's leadership had been quite different. Buchman rarely, if ever, exhorted from the platform. He could be extremely firm, but primarily person to person, and with specific instances in mind.

As he talked with people in America and Canada, and simultaneously looked more closely into his own motivations, Bill faced the fact that one of the strongest drives in human nature is the craving to do well in the eyes of those one puts on a pedestal.

He said many times, 'The hardest battle for me is not to want to please anybody, but simply to say what I mean.'

But he also felt, as a further stage of development, that just speaking up wasn't necessarily the whole answer. If it was done arrogantly, giving the impression that one was right and the other wrong, it could only harden the attitudes. A person had to go deeper than that, seeking to reach an understanding of what the underlying need was.

Bill began to have a growing unease about the hard-line British position with regard to former friends in America, and it turned to alarm when he heard about the recent treatment of several couples who had worked for years with MRA, living in America but British by birth. They made trips to their homeland to visit relatives. During their visits they got on the telephone to old friends, some of whom were currently working with MRA in London or elsewhere, asking to meet up. The suggestion was turned down, so no reunion could take place. This even applied on occasion to close family members.

How could this sort of thing happen? It seemed that in Britain a line had been issued which many were really afraid to go against. One was not to speak to those who apparently had deserted MRA.

By this time Bill realised he was not alone in feeling serious unease that so far there had been no constructive discussion between those in responsible positions on both sides. There had been two meetings, but nothing had been discussed in depth, and the rift remained.

*　　*　　*　　*　　*

By the mid-seventies Bill felt he was quite clear how the division had taken place:

On the parent body side, they had discounted *Up With People* as just a show, and resented its claim to be the next step forward for MRA. They had allowed a situation to arise whereby it was considered disloyal to talk with those supporting *Up With People*. They had stood in judgment on old friends. And many among them truly believed that the best contribution they could make was to maintain and defend the work of MRA around themselves.

On the *Up With People* side, they went all out to establish their programme as the next step, seemingly to forget the concept that had brought many of them into MRA in the first place. They also had many people in their ranks who had suffered from hurts received during the fifties, for whom the show and its popularity was a relief, and yet who still believed in the original change that had come about in their lives through the Oxford Group and MRA.

144

A further thought came into Bill's mind: perhaps the difficulties had needed to happen. Perhaps it was essential to focus the fact that MRA had got off the track before *Sing-Out* was ever thought of. A situation had arisen which might be summed up by saying the world body had become personality-centred instead of God-centred. Buchman himself had warned, 'Don't make MRA your god.'

From the very beginnings of the *Up With People* era, many of Bill's colleagues worldwide had felt their wisest policy was to proceed with the aims and uncompromising standards initiated by Buchman, while trying to learn new and contemporary ways of expressing them. There was, for instance, the continuity of the annual conferences held in Caux, which Bill always attended. There were attractive musical productions touring Europe, Asia and Australasia, with multi-national casts presenting *It's Our Country, Jack!*, *India Arise, Anything To Declare?*, *Wake Up, Matilda* and *Song of Asia*.

Another important element came into the picture.

Bill readily conceded that he had a strong dose of stubbornness in his nature. If he felt something keenly he found it difficult to accept an opposite opinion or to admit he was wrong, although he would eventually and humbly come around to it.

This side of his nature was focused when he heard some views expressed by American friends which shocked and hurt him. He was really concerned to discover that quite a number of people were questioning their faith because of what they heard. His immediate instinct was to defend Buchman's work, as he saw it. But his refusal even to take on board what was being said alienated rather than won quite a few of his former colleagues.

Only later did he come to understand that there were insights to be learnt by him as well as by those who had been caught between *Up With People* and MRA.

In 1975 Bill exchanged letters with one of the senior

Americans who up until that time had supported *Up With People*. They met in New York, at the suggestion of the American. Everything was aired frankly between them, including many of the criticisms and counter-accusations which had flowed both ways across the Atlantic.

These talks seemed to clarify certain things for Bill's friend. He was a senior figure, and although he had at first accepted *Up With People* as the way forward, now found himself drawn back to Buchman's larger concept in which he had been a pioneer.

Several weeks after the talk he telephoned Bill and said, 'I think I may soon have some good news for you.'

Moral Re-Armament was still registered in the USA as a charitable body, with a board of nine directors and offices in New York. The chairman of the board had steadfastly supported *Up With People*, and in 1976 resigned, along with four of his colleagues, with the recommendation that a new board be elected with a majority of members who supported the traditional MRA programme.

This was duly done, and MRA was relaunched in the USA, ten years after the original divisions arose. Others from Britain came to help.

Up With People continued to go from strength to strength, with five casts travelling the world, the liveliness and dynamism of the show continuing to draw enthusiastic audiences. But it was not the concept Buchman had launched on the world.

Bill was now 64 years of age. He felt wiser and humbler and knew he had learnt further important lessons from the last decade. Perhaps, if handled differently, the division need not have happened, yet it was clear to Bill and to many others that some kind of purification had needed to take place, one which strengthened the original concept of MRA's purpose.

Now there was a chance to reassess and rebuild, under a

collective leadership, with no one person in charge, with genuine freedom to air opposing views, so that the right decisions would be taken after frank and open discussion.

XIII

Russia

In 1973 our son Fred entered the Civil Service and acquired a small London flat. In the same year Bill and I took possession of a little red brick house, three up and three down, with casement windows, thirty miles north of London.

The long living room, with floor to ceiling bookshelves on either side of the fireplace, was a perfect place to unpack all our books. For the first time since our marriage, we were able to put all 3,000 of them on shelves. In the end we also lined the walls of an upstairs room with books.

While my collection consisted of some of my childhood favourites, and books on American history from my father's library, as well as the works of Henry James, Bill's books reflected his interests – political biographies, histories of world labour unions and leaders, and an extensive array of books on current affairs.

Along with the books, there were periodicals, magazines, pamphlets and newspapers that came to us from all over the world. Bill carefully read them all as they arrived, made notes on the contents and then stacked them ceiling-high in his office.

Then, as now, there was hardly a political situation in any country with which Bill was not familiar. Coupled with his enormous and unquenchable love for people, this understanding of the issues in the world gave him an immediate meeting point with diplomats, political figures, trade unionists and management men.

'I have always been interested in objective analysis, ever since I was a boy,' Bill said. 'The reason I read so much is because I want to know what is being said and by whom.'

Ever since his East London days Bill had gone out of his way to meet and talk with Communists, to find some point of common interest. In London, in the Ruhr, in travels behind the Iron Curtain to Czechoslovakia in the sixties, he had made every effort to enlist the sincere Communist in a fight for social justice for all classes.

But he was not naïve. Of course there were many Communists who did not accept Bill's approach, because he represented MRA. In many ways Bill was a pioneer, and an influential inspiration to many younger colleagues in later years.

Another such pioneer was Leif Hovelsen, Bill's Norwegian colleague from days in the Ruhr. Starting in the late sixties he met and befriended some of the Russian dissidents who were living in exile from their own homelands, in North America and in Western Europe. He was able to create a bond with many of them because of his own similar experiences in a German concentration camp. These courageous men and women understood MRA because theirs was not a political struggle, but a moral one, based on the search for truth.

*   *   *   *   *

During one of his frequent perambulations around the left-wing bookshops of London, Bill's eye was caught one day by a poster advertising writings by the Novosti Press Agency of Moscow. The charge for an annual subscription was two pounds, and Bill decided on the spot to subscribe for the coming year. He wanted to be informed about the thinking of the Soviet Union, knowing that the Novosti publications would be a mouthpiece of the Soviet government, and that the Press Agency had a close working relationship with the KGB. Brown paper parcels containing five or six small pamphlets from Novosti arrived through our letter box every month for 25 years.

One of the early pamphlets that Bill especially noted was entitled *Man – his ideals and reality* by Eduard Rozental, a graduate of the Moscow Institute for International Relations.

In it Rozental wrote: 'It is impossible to establish universal humaneness on earth by good intentions and persuasion alone. The goal must be achieved by other means .... Marx said that if a man's character was created by circumstances, then it was necessary to make circumstances human. But what does 'human circumstances' mean? They mean the creation of living conditions under which each man can satisfy his needs to the full and develop his talents and abilities.' He went on to describe a chance meeting he had had in Africa with a Frenchman who had spoken passionately to him about Buchman's work of MRA. In his article Rozental dismissed MRA's aims and purposes as naïve.

During the summer of 1968 Eduard Rozental called in, unannounced, at the conference at Caux. He later recalled his encounter at the reception desk:

'The Vice-President for Moral Re-Armament, Daniel Mottu, studied my visiting card with care. Frowning, he tried to remember something ... He remembered.

'"Tell me, didn't you write a book on Moral Re-Armament?"

'"A book – that's saying a lot. A brochure, to be exact."

'"Oh, I am glad you have come."'

Bill was also at Caux at the time, and was more than delighted when he was handed a message saying that a Mr Rozental was in the garden.

Upon receiving Mottu's message, Bill hurried to the terrace tea-garden, to meet the Russian whose writings he had studied. He joined the group as Rozental was speaking,

'Most Christian and other religious sects are limited in their outreach, but Moral Re-Armament has a world outreach. Why? You used to say "Communism or Moral Re-Armament". You have even shed the limitations you had about Communism.'

Bill said he felt it was useless merely to be anti-Communist, and he expressed firmly his convictions that the materialism and selfishness of the so-called free world needed drastic change.

Rozental in turn admitted that though his people were aware that a change was needed in human nature, they had until then not succeeded in achieving it.

The discussion ranged back and forth, and finally, as Rozental prepared to take his leave, he turned to Bill and said, 'You are dangerous; you are convincing; you are gaining!'

A week later Rozental returned to Caux, this time bringing his wife and daughter with him for the weekend.

In January the following year *Izvestia* printed a prize-winning article on MRA by Rozental. The tone was not unfriendly, but it more or less described MRA as superficial and simplistic: 'The dialectic of history demands not reconciliation but the resolution of contradiction. The superior morality must not rock one to sleep, but call to the struggle.'

*   *   *   *   *

During the following years Rozental was based in Geneva as Novosti's correspondent in Switzerland. Daniel Mottu kept in touch with him. After Rozental was given another posting, he left his Moscow address with Mottu so that they could keep in touch.

In 1985 Rozental wrote a book about various movements in the West that appealed to younger people, entitled *Paradox of Protests*. In it he again attacked MRA quite strongly.

Two years later Rozental returned to Novosti Press as a 'political observer'. In 1988 Mottu invited him to come to Caux again. However, the Russian was prevented from accepting the invitation by order of his superior, who was deeply suspicious of MRA.

Rozental regretted that he was unable to make the visit, but wrote to Mottu: 'I am in complete agreement with you on the need of an international dialogue aiming at mutual understanding in our ever more interdependent world. If you have a concrete proposal to provide for a new exchange of views in the context of the present world situation and can elaborate a common programme aiming at consolidating human morality and the cause of peace, we are open to this.'

The following summer, after a replacement of his superior at Novosti, Rozental did visit Caux again. He was not the only person from the USSR to visit the MRA conference that summer, as the dissident philosopher and writer, Vladimir Zelinsky, came with his family, following a visit to Moscow by Leif Hovelsen and Bryan Hamlin, a younger British colleague based in the United States, who had been greatly inspired and encouraged by Bill's interest in the people and issues of the Soviet Union.

After Rozental's visit to Caux a new edition of his book on Western youth movements was published in 1990. Bill found the critical reference to MRA had been dropped from the new edition, re-entitled *This eternal theme*.

*　　*　　*　　*　　*

On November 9, 1989, Bill and I sat in our living room, trying to absorb the news that the Berlin Wall was coming down. Our emotions were as turbulent as those we had experienced in 1945 when news came of the end of World

War II. This November day marked the end of the Cold War, which Bill had lived with for much of his adult life.

Bill began to feel he would like to make a trip to Russia himself. Over the years at the ILO and elsewhere he had met many from the Soviet Union. Even at the advanced age of 77 he felt the deep desire to visit the part of the world about which he had studied so much, and whose people he had always met with warmth and high hopes.

During the 1989 Caux summer conference, three months earlier, Bill and I had been introduced by Daniel Mottu to the Russian Press Attaché in Geneva, Vladimir Shebanov. Shebanov, an immensely tall man, fluent in English, had visited Caux the previous year, as the Soviet Ambassador's representative on the occasion of MRA's 50th anniversary, and had been impressed with the atmosphere he sensed there. He had remarked to Mottu on the look of enjoyment on the faces of the conference delegates, some of whom he found at work in the kitchen and serving the meals.

When he returned to Caux the following year, Vladimir Shebanov brought his father and mother. As we met them, Bill and I for the first time established a warm rapport with a Russian family.

Bill sought Daniel Mottu's advice about his own hopes of a visit to Moscow, and at Mottu's suggestion asked Jean-Jacques Odier, a Swiss with a keen interest in labour union matters, to accompany him there. It was necessary to be able to converse in either French or German as well as English in Moscow. Odier delightedly agreed, and they made plans for a ten-day visit in April, 1990.

At that time the whole western world seemed to be heading for Russia, and Bill was one of many who queued for many hours outside the Russian embassy to get his visa.

Some private visits to the Soviet Union had been made by MRA colleagues. A Finnish businessman had been there on numerous occasions in connection with his work. In the

154

course of his visits to Leningrad he began to inform people about the aims and work of MRA. Leif Hovelsen made his own first visit to Moscow in 1989.

Bill and Odier found the Russian people very warm-hearted. At the same time there were problems of bureaucracy. For example, on arrival at the airport, one collected one's luggage and looked around for a trolley on which to wheel it through Customs. The only way to get a trolley was by paying roubles, and roubles could only be obtained the other side of the Customs barrier!

As they left Moscow airport, on their way into the city itself, over 400 army tanks and gun carriers were on the main avenue, rehearsing for the May victory parade when the Russians commemorate the end of what they call the 'Great Patriotic War'.

Gorbachev had just withdrawn the 'right to work' legislation. Under that legislation, ever since the 1930s the Soviet Union was able to have zero unemployment, and had found a job of some sort for everyone, which might include street sweeping or being sent to the far north to work there. With the withdrawal of that 'right to work', and because of the low levels of productivity and the move towards the market economy, prices of food, goods and raw materials were increasing sharply, and unemployment was rising. Before 1990 trade union leaders were usually government officials, not held in very high regard by the workers. In the course of 1990-91 genuine trade unions started to spring up and even organise strikes, protesting about the rising cost of living, and the growing levels of unemployment.

Bill and Odier were received by the International Department of the All-Soviet Union Central Council of Trade Unions, which had 142 million members, and whose head Bill had met at the ILO the previous year. They met the Director of the International Section of the Russian Trade Unions, and his deputy whom Bill had also met at the ILO.

Alexander Shebanov, the father of Vladimir Shebanov,

whom Bill and I had met at Caux, belonged to the Institute of World Economy and International Relations, in the Academy of Sciences. He arranged for Bill and Odier to speak about Moral Re-Armament's work to 19 heads of department, representing many Asian and European countries, at the Institute. In the course of an hour and a half many wide-ranging questions were discussed, such as, 'Has not the time come now for both economists and governments to take seriously the need of the moral factor?' and 'How do you relate Moral Re-Armament to world politics?'

On their final night in Moscow Bill and Odier were given a wonderful dinner in the Shebanov home, and invited to return with their wives.

*   *   *   *   *

After Bill and Odier's visit to Moscow in April, 1990, Bill and I were again at Caux for the summer conference. Eduard Rozental had been away when they were in Moscow, so Bill was most interested to hear from Daniel Mottu that Rozental had accepted an invitation to visit Caux again, and would be bringing with him another man from Novosti Press.

At a seminar held at the conference to inform delegates on the current situation in Russia, Rozental began by apologising to Mottu for the critical things he had said about MRA in the past. He had, he said, been wrong about it. He spoke without notes, quite at ease, and skilfully summarised the issues the world was facing with so many vast changes taking place.

In January, 1991, Novosti Press put out a fresh press release written by Rozental, explaining why he had changed his attitude about MRA. Under the title, *We found a common language*, the article concluded:

'It would be wrong to think that the plenary sessions and round tables go on in Caux in an oily setting, where everyone agrees with one another. Often quite heated discussions come up, which do not always end in a consensus and opponents remain with their own convictions. Which does not prevent – and this is perhaps the most important thing – a respectful attitude to the other's opinion. Is that not the main mark of civilised behaviour?

'And I state that in spite of differences, all of us, Soviet, English, Swiss, French, American, Brazilian and other participants in this conference, have found a common language on the basis of generally accepted values which have no boundary. And this is the main positive sign of our contacts with Moral Re-Armament, which I am absolutely certain will continue to develop.'

This press release was the first positive assessment of MRA in the Soviet media. It was carried by several provincial Soviet papers, and in that same last year of the old USSR there were other articles which publicised in a positive light the work that MRA was seeking to do.

In September, 1991, the Moscow-based monthly journal *Druzhba Narodov* (Friendship of Peoples) published a 14-page article by Bryan Hamlin on Moral Re-Armament's work in the world, entitled *Forgiveness in international affairs.*

*   *   *   *   *

Another Russian whom Bill and I met at Caux was Dr Bella Gribkova from Gorky. Bill and I met her for luncheon on the Caux terrace on a sunny summer day. A lovely young woman greeted us, dressed in blue jeans, with a mane of long, curly, light-brown hair sweeping over one shoulder.

She told us about her work as a lecturer in English at the University of Gorky, about her husband who was a pianist and about their young son.

At that first brief meeting we both sensed in Bella a warm human being, quite candid and forthcoming, who over-arched ideology. Communication was instant and without effort, and we found it most interesting and helpful to learn from her what someone who had grown up in the Communist world really felt about a number of things.

The following year she made a visit to England, and these are some of the comments she made:

'I love my country and at the same time am sorry for it. There is a great deal of difference between the adjectives "Russian" and "Soviet". We were able to get rid of the shackles of Communism because the Russian soul in us has survived.

'Historically the Russian people are very religious. The fact that our faith has survived and helped us was due greatly to the influence of the babushkas, or grandmothers.

'My father worked in a steelworks and my mother also worked full time. So I was really brought up by my grand-mother, like many others. She used to read to me from a shabby little book with no title. Only later I discovered it was the New Testament. She also secretly christened me, without my parents knowing. They were part of the system and believed in Communism. But they were high-minded people who thought it right simply to strive for excellence in character rather than personal comfort. My mother used to say that if you allow yourself to want things, there is no end to it. You always want more.

'We are in debt to the world because of what our system has done to various countries. I think we will find strength to make up for this. One of the crucial concepts of the Orthodox faith is sin. All our people need to be aware of it and to repent. The whole country is undergoing it, and I hope that it will be a new stage in our development.'

*   *   *   *   *

In the next years almost 50 of Bill's colleagues made trips to countries of the former Soviet Union, several learning the Russian language.

In the summer of 1991, 107 from the USSR came to the Caux summer conference. Delegations also came from

Rumania, Czechoslovakia, Bulgaria, Poland, Hungary and the Baltic States. Most were neither dissident nor Communist, but represented the general population who at that stage wanted to see changes and more freedom in their countries.

More recently, in Sweden and Denmark MRA colleagues played host to seminars involving dialogue between people from the Baltic states and their Russian neighbours, about their difficult relationships.

In November, 1994, a delegation of eight Members of Parliament from Kiev, in the Ukraine, came to Britain for ten days, to find out how to make democracy work. They came under the auspices of *Foundations for Freedom*, an MRA initiative, meeting individuals at all levels of national life, including Members of Parliament.

Experience of recent years shows that nations who have recently regained their democratic freedom are more than ready to understand Moral Re-Armament – as a concept so clearly outlined by Bill. It could be applied to every country, every political system, every religion, if rightly understood; not as a movement to join, concentrating on personal conduct alone, but as an idea that could give direction to a nation.

Bill's work of studying the political and ideological situations, and of caring passionately about the people involved in them, created the bedrock upon which many of his younger colleagues were able to build. His open-heartedness and his informed evaluations served as an example to many.

32 In Tiananmen Square, Beijing, with Ruan Kekong, a CAFIU translator. In the distance is the Great Hall of the People.

33 With miners coming off shift at Tangshan, centre of the coal-mining area where a devastating earthquake occurred in 1976.

34 In the Great Hall of the People, Zhu Xuefan gives a banquet for Bill Jaeger, an old friend he had not seen for 40 years.

35 Joan Jaeger, wife of Frederic   36 Frederic Jaeger

37 Bill and Clara Jaeger at Knebworth

XIV

China

In 1973 many of the world's papers carried articles about the changes taking place in China after the death of Mao Zedong. A representative of the United Nations stated, 'In China in the next 30 to 40 years you will see the most drastic shift in the world balance of economic power for many centuries.'

Bill had often wondered what had happened to his friend Zhu Xuefan, since their first meeting at the Philadelphia ILO conference in 1944. Bill did not know, even, if he had survived the Cultural Revolution. He had not written him over the past years, not wanting to endanger his friend in any way. Simply receiving a letter with a foreign stamp might have done so. During the Mao years China had not been represented at the ILO, so it had not been possible for Bill to get news of Zhu Xuefan.

In New York one day in 1977, Bill had the thought to go to the Public Library and to look in the Chinese records in the Public Affairs section and see if Zhu Xuefan was listed. Within five minutes he found his name and address. He was still the Minister of Communications in the cabinet.

Finding the name so easily moved Bill very much. 'I believe in one thing leading to another,' he said, 'and I believe in a sense of direction, of being led. I believe in that with all I have got. It is all connected with meeting people.

161

You are led to the right people at the right time.'

In the New Year he wrote to Zhu Xuefan, sending him greetings and asking how he was. To his great joy he received a letter in return, sending best wishes. This was the beginning of a correspondence, in which Bill was able to inform Zhu Xuefan about what he was doing.

In 1982 China was once again represented at the ILO in Geneva, with a delegation of over 50. Bill met some of them, and was touched to hear that many of them had been told by Zhu Xuefan specifically to look out for him.

In 1985, Zhu Xuefan asked Bill to send him some information about MRA, having been invited by Bill to an MRA conference in Washington. Unfortunately he was not well enough to make the journey.

Zhu Xuefan at that time was Vice-Chairman of the Standing Committee of the National People's Congress of China, Chairman of the Revolutionary Committee of the Kuomintang, and Vice-President of the Chinese Association for International Understanding (CAFIU).

In his next letter Bill said that he would like to make a visit to China, to renew their friendship, and that, if such a visit were possible, he would like to bring an American colleague with him – Richard Ruffin, executive director of MRA in America.

In response Bill had a letter from the Secretary-General of CAFIU, sent at the request of Zhu Xuefan, inviting Bill for a ten-day visit to Beijing, Shanghai and other Chinese cities in the spring of 1986. Bill accepted, with joy, and then received a further personal letter from Zhu Xuefan, looking forward to the visit and to renewing their friendship.

*   *   *   *   *

Bill and Ruffin were met at Beijing airport in March, 1986, and taken to a charming guest house which had been put at their disposal by CAFIU. That evening they were driven, in a Russian-made car with curtained windows, to the Great Hall of the People in Tiananmen Square. Zhu Xuefan was standing on the steps of the famous building, waiting for them. It was a moving moment for them both, as they went towards each other with open arms. It had been 42 years since they met.

Inside they met other invited guests, and found a banquet had been laid out for them. Many courses were served, many toasts drunk in orange juice and soda water, and gifts were exchanged. Bill was given a magnificent scarlet silk tablecloth, embroidered with birds and flowers, so large it was able to hang as a curtain in our English home.

After the meal the speeches began with a welcome from the Chinese hosts. When Bill replied, he began by emphasising how sorry he was, as an Englishman, for Britain's treatment of China during the Boxer Rebellion and for the way the British had provoked the Opium War. He told his hosts about his first meeting with Zhu Xuefan in America, and introduced Ruffin – a man sensitive to the fact that he represented a Big Power, not always popular in certain parts of the world. Ruffin said that he was born a Southerner, in a professional family, and that until he met Bill and his friends he had never had real conversations with either blacks or trade unionists.

After his return to England, Bill reported to Ambassador Ji Chaozhu at the Chinese Embassy in London about his trip. Ambassador Ji, a gracious and courteous diplomat, had been brought up and educated in America, returning to China at the time of the Korean War. He acted as interpreter for both Zhou Enlai and Mao Zedong before being given diplomatic postings. After his term as ambassador in London he became a Deputy Secretary General of the United Nations in New York.

In the spring of 1989 Bill wondered if he might invite Ambassador Ji and his wife, with some of their staff, to the British MRA conference centre in Cheshire, for a country house weekend in a large English home set in beautiful landscaped gardens.

Bill was 77 years of age, and in keeping with his life's aim to build a team and to include other people in all he was doing, he asked James Hore-Ruthven, a younger colleague based in London, if he would go with him to the Chinese Embassy to invite the ambassador. James agreed.

The visit was arranged, and the ambassador said he would indeed like to bring a number of his staff with him.

Among those invited to MRA's Cheshire centre to meet the Chinese guests were the Lord Mayor of Liverpool, British industrialists from the area, A R K Mackenzie, a former British Ambassador, and representatives from the many spheres of British life in which MRA was at work.

The weekend went off with great style. Everyone soon seemed at home in the welcoming atmosphere. On the last morning Ambassador Ji prepared to speak to the hundred or so people who were gathered there. Standing in front of a brightly burning log fire in the oak-beamed hall, he looked at his audience, and then put down the sheets of paper in his hand, saying, 'I am not going to use this speech I prepared. I want to speak to you from my heart.'

With great skill and humour he presented 5,000 years of Chinese civilisation and 4,000 years of recorded history, concluding with a look 200 years into the future – a vast sweep. He reminded his listeners that China had invented paper, movable type, gunpowder and bureaucracy, but she had fallen behind because of a policy of closing the doors to the outside world. 'But,' he went on, 'we are extroverts, we like life and friends and laughter.'

He described vividly his own harrowing experiences during the Cultural Revolution. He said it was a very difficult time. In the past China had been a secretive society, which only encouraged bureaucracy and the misuse of power. Now they needed to practise transparency. He spoke about building the new society in China.

Ambassador Ji said, 'The spirit of moral re-armament is essential in ensuring the success of our reforms. A major part of these reforms is opening the windows to the outside world. When the windows are open, flies come in. Because of that China needs Moral Re-Armament, just as the whole world needs Moral Re-Armament.'

*   *   *   *   *

Bill was often invited to functions at the Chinese Embassy, including the annual reception to mark the revolution of 1949.

He realised you could no more plan for the twenty-first century without China than you could plan for Europe in 1946 without Germany. He wondered what the future held for China; why had things gone wrong in Tiananmen Square? Was it fear of a second cultural revolution and further internal civil war? Was anarchy something to be feared above all else by those in charge of one and a quarter billion people? Bill felt it was important that the rest of the world accurately understood what was really going on in China, and what they were faced with in the coming months.

He suggested to Ambassador Ji that it might be helpful to hold a seminar at the Chinese Embassy, where he and some of his MRA colleagues could describe the work they were doing, and some of the embassy staff could speak about their thoughts for China's future.

The ambassador agreed to the plan, and Bill took a group of 20 with him to the Embassy in October, 1989. It was a memorable moment when the party approached the imposing building in Portland Place and rang the bell. The seminar in the Embassy was taking place not long after the events in Tiananmen Square, and the building had been under constant picketing.

The party were ushered up the wide, red-carpeted stairs, where they were received by Mme Zhang Youyun, who had interpreted for Queen Elizabeth II on her visit to China a few years previously, and Mr Tan Ronggen, first secretary in the Embassy. Mr Tan had attended several

165

MRA functions in London, and came to tea in our home in Hertfordshire, along with several of the younger embassy staff.

For an hour speeches were exchanged about the future of China in the modern world, and experiences were detailed of what MRA had meant in the lives of some of the visitors. Ambassador Ji and his wife joined them, and when that part of the evening ended they ushered their guests into a large adjoining room, where a magnificent buffet meal was laid out, and tables arranged so that informal discussions could continue. Such gatherings – and they were continued by Ambassador Ji's successor, Ambassador Ma Yuzhen – took place without any publicity on either side. At a time when official diplomatic relations between London and Beijing were strained, and when much of the media were dramatising the issues on which the two countries diverged, they helped to lay a foundation of friendship and trust on which more constructive international relationships could later be built.

In April, 1991, Bill made another trip to China, as part of a British group representing MRA, invited by the Chinese Association for International Understanding. The group with Bill comprised former Ambassador A R K Mackenzie, James Hore-Ruthven from London, and Jim Wigan, a man from a farming background, who had been host to Ambassador Ji and his staff at the country house weekend in Cheshire.

The party was received in the Great Hall of the People by Hou Jingru, Vice-Chairman of the Chinese People's Political Consultative Conference (equivalent to the British House of Lords, the visitors were told!), who said to them, 'Without moral progress, economic and social progress is impossible.'

They were given six banquets by national and regional officials, including the Minister of Labour. They met managers, trade union and civic leaders, educators and university professors, farmers and Christian clergy.

Amongst the places the delegation visited was the northern city of Tangshan, centre of a coalmining area, where in a terrible earthquake in 1976, 250,000 people lost their lives. The extent of the damage was never realised internationally. The Chinese Government drafted in hundreds of thousands of troops to help with the rescue.

Bill had animated and moving discussions with local coalminers coming off their shift. They recounted in detail the suffering and devastation in 1976. The Deputy Mayor of the city, a distinguished woman who had lost her only daughter in the earthquake, responded so deeply to the contacts with Bill and his friends that she came personally to the international MRA conference in Caux later in the year.

In Beijing the delegation were taken to visit all the principal cultural sights, including the New Summer Palace. This is a vast and beautiful park, laid out by the last Empress, with lakes and ornamental bridges and gardens. However, at the suggestion of Ambassador Mackenzie, the delegation also asked to be taken to the Old Summer Palace. This request at first was the cause for some puzzlement among their hosts, as the Old Summer Palace is not on the normal tourist round, but it was eventually added to the programme.

The Old Summer Palace, built in the seventeenth and eighteenth centuries in a remarkable blend of Chinese and European styles, had been one of the wonders of China, but it was looted and burned down by the British and French forces under Lord Elgin at the culmination of the Opium Wars in 1860. Amidst the impressive ruins Ambassador Mackenzie said a few words, and the delegation stood for a moment in silent respect and penitence for what had been done in Britain's name.

This was an important healing gesture, for, as Bill discovered, the story of British and French destructiveness still has a prominent place in Chinese schoolbooks.

After this, similar exchange visits began to take place regularly between China and Britain, with groups from industry and education going to each others' countries. Quite a number of Bill's younger colleagues joined in the same adventure, following the steps already taken and finding new ones.

China is seeking to go through, in a single century, many of the reforms that took seven or eight centuries in Europe. Bill was very touched when one of the Chinese government said to him, 'We will never forget the way you remained a friend of China at the difficult time of Tiananmen Square, when no one else would speak to us.'

One Chinese trade union leader said to a group of MRA guests, 'Your visit has given guidance to us. Moral Re-Armament is a common cause for all mankind.'

In conversations with people in Britain Bill often said, 'We can learn so much from the Chinese.' He would quote Premier Zhou Enlai, 'A good leader must unite with comrades whom he dislikes. We must have faith in comrades with shortcomings. We are willing to cooperate with all countries that treat us as equals. Dogma will never change China. It must be by productivity and education, based on ethical values.'

Bill made regular enquiries about his old friend Zhu Xuefan, who suffered more and more from ill-health. Bill never ceased to be grateful to him, for the way he introduced him to China. He felt he had been led, person by person into a vast, unknown territory. By virtue of the warm friendships he made with some remarkable Chinese, he could at least offer a possible way forward through what might be a minefield of difficulties.

'I do believe in China,' Bill said once, 'and in what China can do for the world in the next decades.'

XV

Today and tomorrow

In April, 1992, Bill reached his 80th birthday. He could properly be called a father-figure now, someone always ready to listen, to ask sensitive questions that could draw out people's deeper thoughts. Young and old alike approach him when he comes on the scene, enjoying talking with him.

As it always has been, his daily programme is based around people to meet and be in touch with, and new people he has never met before, but whose names have come to his attention through reading, for instance. Equally he spends time in writing to friends all over the world, sending them some of the latest information and documentation he feels might interest or be of help to them.

He so often says, when considering what to do, who to see, or whether to make a certain trip, '...for his sake', '...for her sake'. That is the deciding factor.

I know that some people think an ideal marriage is one where there are no fights. I'm not sure I agree. It may be possible where one partner is the dominant character and the other is happy to defer, and even think the stronger character is probably right. But Bill and I are both very strong characters, with strong wills – though the self-will may take different forms. On the whole, I think I am probably the more difficult character to live with,

169

especially when I retreat into a world of my own and nurse my hurts in silence.

I sometimes feel, and I've been told by one or two of Bill's colleagues, that he can sometimes over-state in giving a report on one of his experiences. It occasionally sounds to me that he is so keen to make a point that he can over-emphasise. I have tried at times to contradict him on this, but he usually ends up proving to me that what he said was correct.

Gordon Wise told me once, 'Bill quoted something so-and-so said, and when we showed that the man did not exactly say that, Bill replied, "Yes, but it was what he meant to say."'

Gordon also says, 'There are many apocryphal stories about Bill, like the one when, at a reception, he met an Asian gentleman. By way of introduction Bill said, "I know your Foreign Minister." The gentleman replied, "I am the Foreign Minister." "Exactly!" said Bill.'

Yes, we have ding-dongs. Bill is no longer afraid of my reactions and very quickly tells me when he thinks I am wrong about something. Usually I can accept that, and his objectivity can be helpful because I can still be too personally involved in the way I evaluate situations.

But Bill has often said that he feels one of his sins is in being too self-sufficient. And he does have a large helping of Anglo-German stubbornness in his make-up. Sometimes when I come up against this, like a wall I can't get through, and he won't listen to me, I can react in real hot anger. Usually it is when he is convinced about something, and I am not. I feel disappointed that we can't have a free discussion, and sometimes I give my own views so strongly that we both feel unhappy and sad afterwards. But it doesn't last, because we love each other so much, and usually he is the one to say sorry first.

'The older I get,' Bill said recently, 'the more I feel that I can find a place where I am wrong somewhere, and I can start there.'

There was a time when Bill and I found it difficult to contradict strong personalities whom we also respected. Equally, I sometimes think it may not have been easy for Bill's colleagues to disagree openly with him. When he has a deeply held view, Bill can be tempted to talk down any opposition.

What we both love, more than almost anything else, is having people to our home; to make them feel welcome, to feed them nice food and especially to enter into lively discussions about subjects that will stir and stimulate debate. These can go on for hours, perhaps on subjects that people have not known how to discuss before.

And along with all these many friends, there is a constant exchange of news and views with our son, now very much on a common wavelength.

Fred took up a career in the Central Management of the Civil Service, and now works in the Cabinet Office. He was recently part of a small team in the unit supporting the Prime Minister's Adviser on Efficiency, whose report with recommendations to improve resources management systems across government was published in May, 1995.

Earlier in his career he also had a spell as assistant private secretary to the Leader of the House of Lords and the Government Chief Whip in the House of Lords.

In 1981, Fred married Joan Gaskell who is now head of the School of Literary and Media Studies in the University of North London. They have bought a seventeenth century cottage in Kent, where Bill and I have spent many happy weekends and Christmas holidays in the lovely countryside.

*   *   *   *   *

In our home, even though there is so much printed matter every day – papers, magazines, incoming letters, articles to be filed for reference, Bill is extremely neat – much neater than I am. He never leaves anything lying around, and keeps his papers in tidy piles.

He hates losing things, or misplacing them rather, since

we have only ever lost one book out of the 4,000 in our small house. But his first reaction if something is not readily to hand is to suggest that he gave the lost object, or letter, or piece of paper to me, so please could I find it? Sometimes this used to irk me, but now I just smile to myself, search my papers and wait for it to turn up in his own den, which must house over a million pieces of paper, hundreds of folders, several hundred books and maybe 50 cases full of documents. He has his own filing system, and can put his hand on any important document in it.

We have travelled for so much of our married life – 47 years now – and packing has had its moments of friction. Nowadays I put in his clothes and let him fill in with books, papers, folders full of data he may want to use. If he is going off somewhere there are often last-minute messages to be delivered, letters to sign, things to be followed through that have piled up. I am on hand through all this, and after he has gone I go to the post office to mail the letters. When the taxi comes to take him to the airport or the station we share a hurried kiss, and he is gone, once again.

Then I am able to sink down in a chair and catch my breath, and realise that I have some free time to pick up the pieces and get all back in order. It is a relief.

But, along with the relief, there is nowadays another emotion: is he doing too much for his strength? Will this husband of mine, with his tremendous will and drive and determination to carry on seeing so many people, damage his health in some serious way? Will he return safe to me?

*   *   *   *   *

In the summer of 1991 Bill had some drastic dental work done, with many teeth removed and a new plate made. His mouth became quite tender and sore over the next 18 months, and finally he was given some strong tablets by a specialist in London, to try and ease the discomfort. These tablets made him feel so ill that he made an appointment to see our own local doctor.

172

I went in to the surgery with Bill, and he explained about the tablets. The doctor took his blood pressure and listened to his heart beat. He straightened up and looked at him. 'I want to get you to the hospital', he said. He got on the phone straight away, arranging for Bill to be admitted.

It all happened so suddenly we could hardly take it in. Our dear friend and neighbour, Angela Owbridge, had driven us to the surgery and now drove us the three miles to the local hospital. They were all ready for him there, and he was quickly put in a cubicle and wired up to machines that monitored his heartbeat.

I waited outside in the corridor, and several hours later he was moved to one of the two private rooms on the ward.

Then began five days of waiting and not knowing. We heard on the second day that he was to be moved in the next few days to Harefield, the country's leading heart hospital, where he would be given a heart pacemaker.

It was a real shock to both of us – a bolt from the blue. It was such a shock that on the first night when I returned to our little home I broke down and cried out to God that I couldn't bear to lose Bill.

I spent every one of those first five days sitting beside his bed, watching the green lines dancing across the monitoring machine, darting sometimes up, sometimes down. On the third day Bill asked me to jot down some thoughts he had for his younger colleagues, and for the future of MRA. Then he read to me from St Paul, from 15th Corinthians: 'Therefore my beloved brethren, be ye steadfast, unmovable, always abounding in the work of the Lord, forasmuch as ye know that your labour is not in vain in the Lord.'

Actually, Bill didn't slow down one bit, propped up in his hospital bed. He would talk to everyone who came into his room – how were they? where were they from? He told them about his own life work and offered his own analysis of the current news. It was a busy ward and, even though his room was in a kind of alcove, Bill became a vital part of all that went on in it.

Counting as usual, he said he got to know 40 nurses of different stages of seniority, plus the ladies who brought his meals, made his bed and cleaned the room. Several of the nurses, as they passed by in the course of their duties, would come and ask Bill questions, sitting on the end of his bed and wanting to talk. And of course the man who brought the newspapers round each day suddenly found his business booming, as Bill pounced on his selection and chose freely from it.

On the fifth day in the local hospital we were told that an ambulance would be taking Bill to Harefield later that day. I brought a small overnight case with me, in case I could hitch a ride in the ambulance and go along with him.

When it had been dark for quite some time outside, suddenly there they were in the doorway – two uniformed paramedics with a stretcher. They were wonderfully caring and skilful, as they lifted Bill up and strapped him in, and we were off down the long corridors to the front door, me tagging along behind, not knowing yet if they would take me.

After Bill was lifted into the ambulance and made comfortable they turned to me and said, 'You too,' and I jumped inside.

We were accompanied by one of the nurses who had been looking after Bill and who carried all his records. The lady paramedic got into the driver's seat, the man strapped Bill up to a monitoring machine and put an oxygen mask over his face. The nurse and I sat on the long seat opposite, and we were off, in a swirl of flashing lights.

The medic stood over Bill, keeping an eye on the flickering green lines that registered his heartbeat, every once in a while putting the oxygen mask over his face.

I never took my eyes off Bill. I was so moved to see him lying there, looking every one of his 80 years.

It took an hour to reach Harefield in the middle of the evening traffic. Once there we found all in readiness for him, in a large ward. The operation to fit the pacemaker was to be early the next morning. I kissed him goodnight and found my way to the hospital's guesthouse.

As I rang for the elevator the next morning about nine o'clock, the doors opened, and there was Bill, being wheeled by an orderly on his way to the operating theatre. Some timing!

I went up to his ward, and sat waiting for him. Less than an hour later Bill was wheeled in, half propped up and smiling at me.

'I had no pain at all,' Bill told me, 'it was a local anaesthetic, and it only took 45 minutes.'

To my great astonishment he was given a hot meal an hour later, which he tackled as if nothing had happened.

He was kept in hospital overnight, and 36 hours later he was tucked up in his own bed at home. We both said prayers of humble gratitude to God.

During those days in hospital, Bill was tremendously impressed with the dedication and spirit of all the doctors, nurses, orderlies and volunteer women who looked after him. This was Britain's National Health Service at its first-class best. Bill wrote letters to almost all of them later, to thank them for their care of him.

As I write this book, Bill is 83, and finding much to enjoy in life. And his pacemaker is managing to keep up with his unflagging determination to meet and make friends with people wherever and whenever he can. Besides reading, seeing his friends and meeting people at functions, Bill thoroughly enjoys watching television.

Football is high on the list, and every Saturday afternoon all the scores have to be noted. Stockport County and West Ham United are still his favourites, along with Nottingham Forest. He is very keen on cricket as well.

He can be deeply moved by hearing hymns sung on the Sunday programmes, and beats time with his hands as if conducting. Anything from Beethoven stirs him, and all choirs, taking him back to those childhood roots and the music which brought healing and balm into the lives of his parents and the working class folk of the mill towns.

*   *   *   *   *

The last word is his:

'I am not interested in getting people to join something. The point is to get an idea into people, whatever their background, to help them to begin with themselves. You have to have great patience, and great care and compassion, to help each individual to become responsible. And you must always have a vision for what people can become.

'I have learned not to hurt people. I made my choice to commit myself to and learn from people. My work with people has not been just to make friends on the superficial level. There has been the depth of understanding and addressing the needs in people. It is important not to use people.

'We have the greatest task in history, and we've got to think for the whole world. Bitter men can never unite people. Selfish men can never bring about a society that is above class. And people who don't live what they talk about will never capture the hearts and minds of the next generation. Our commitment must be to God, and not just to moral standards – and we must make sure that our families know we mean it.

'I feel our task is only beginning really. We've got the next 10, 20, 30 years to do something that's effective. It's a great chance we have.'

Bibliography

Battiscombe, Georgina Shaftesbury *A Biography of the Seventh Earl*, Constable, 1974

Engels, Friedrich *The Condition of the Working Class in England*

Grogan, William *John Riffe of the Steelworkers*, Coward–McCann, 1959

Hovelsen, Leif *Out of the Evil Night*, Blandford Press, 1959

The ILO and the World of Work, International Labour Office, 1984

The International Labour Organisation Backgrounder, prepared by the ILO Bureau of Public Information, 1991

Nobel Peace Prize, 1969 (David Morse), The ILO, 1969

The Acceptance Speech on the Occasion of the Award of the Nobel Peace Prize, Oslo, December 10, 1969

Lean, Garth *Frank Buchman – A Life*, Constable, 1985

Moral Re-Armament *The Fight To Serve*, 1943

Rozental, Eduard *Man – His Ideals and Reality*, Novosti
Press Agency Publishing House, 1967

Suyin, Han *Eldest Son, Zhou Enlai and the Making of
Modern China*, Jonathan Cape, 1993

Twitchell, Kenaston *Regeneration in the Ruhr*, Princeton
University Press, 1981

Uglow, Jenny *Elizabeth Gaskell*, Faber & Faber, 1993

also by Clara Jaeger:

Annie, Grosvenor Books, 1968

Philadelphia Rebel, Grosvenor Books, 1988

Index

Photo credits

From the Jaeger family collection: 2, 11, 19, 26, 28, 29, 31, 32, 34, 35

From a water-colour painting by Peter Sutcliffe: 27

Michael Blundell: 20

David Channer: 36

R N Haile: 5

MRA Archive: 6, 10, 12, 21, 25, 30

Arthur Strong: 1, 3, 4, 7, 8, 9, 13, 14, 15, 16, 17, 22, 23, 24

Signe Lund Strong: 18

Jim Wigan: 33

Picture layouts: Peter Sisam